This book is dedicated,
to my father
Dennis Williams

and to the memory of my mother
Florence Webster Williams

with love, and with gratitude
for a conscious policy of encouraging us
to find and fulfil our own creative potential
— and for being good people.

Moon Over Water
The Path of Meditation

Jesssica Macbeth

Foreword by Pat Pilkington

Gateway

Gateway
an imprint of
Gill & Macmillan Ltd
Hume Avenue
Park West
Dublin 12
with associated companies throughout the world
www.gillmacmillan.ie

© *1990 Jessica Macbeth*
0 7171 3389 3
Printed by ColourBooks Ltd, Dublin
Set in 11 on 13 pt Bembo,
by Action Typesetting of Gloucester

The paper used in this book is made from the wood
pulp of managed forests. For every tree felled, at least one
tree is planted, thereby renewing natural resources.

A catalogue record is available for this book
from the British Library.

9 10

Table of Contents

Part IX: On the Wings of Transformation 141

The psychology of transformation. Meditation and the healing of the psyche.

Part X: On Ascending the Mountain 155

Religion, spirituality and meditation. Some meditation exercises. A non-definition of enlightenment.

Appendix A 172

Twenty meditation techniques.

Appendix B 178

Table showing qualities of each meditation technique in Appendix A.

Notes, References, Tapes: 180

Foreword

This book is about learning to love ourselves. It is about taking time daily to calm the turbulence of mind and emotion; of letting go our defences and finding a balanced path into our inner world. As Jessica Macbeth says "meditation is not something we do in our heads; it is something we do with our whole selves — body, mind, emotions and spirit, and it affects us on all those levels". Meditation gives us something that in our present day stressful lifestyle we don't readily have: a chance to sit with ourselves, as integrated and earthed as a mountain, "awake, alert and utterly solid". It takes us beyond psychological function and shifts something deep within us. It is part of any well-rounded life.

It has been very heartening to learn that in recent years an increasing number of doctors have been recommending relaxation and meditation for patients suffering from stress. It has taken away the 'hippie' image left over from the sixties and encouraged many of us to have a go for ourselves. The trouble is that, without a good teacher we often get discouraged, and like many another, I have experienced very great difficulty in focusing and calming my all-too-active mind. Fifteen minutes of failure is pretty depressing, and it was not until Jessica Macbeth became my teacher that I began to inch my way forward.

To start with I was encouraged to practise for only five minutes at a time — simply counting the breath, not to wait until I could do it 'properly'. "Meditation in itself helps us to be more earthed and centred. Being more earthed and centred helps us practise meditation". Next I learned a calming exercise that could be undertaken anywhere, even in a committee meeting or on a crowded train — just focusing relaxed attention on a thumb nail! So simple, and always available.

The great surprise to me was that it worked! It produced almost immediate results. For someone used to *doing* rather than *being*, this was a considerable surprise and quite a shock. Things were changing in and around me and I was both astonished and increasingly excited to find this way of living more comfortably with myself. It came, I might add, in the nick of time as pressure increased for all of us involved with the expanding work of the Bristol Cancer Help Centre.

Over the last decade I have been privileged to witness the extraordinary way in which our patients at the Cancer Help Centre turn themselves around spiritually, psychologically, and very often physically as they work with the 'Bristol Programme' of self-healing. Facing a life-threatening illness plays havoc with normal coping systems, and the first thing that gets washed overboard is peace of mind. We have seen, over and over, the restorative influence of meditation: of finding the true self in the depths of being we hardly knew existed; experiencing the relief which comes from finding soul-rest.

To begin with there is a noticeable calming and balancing of consciousness, and then an extraordinary expansion. An awakening as if from many years of sleep. We have seen the 'sleeping beauty' legend enacted over and over as patients discover who they really are, and find the music of their lives. Sometimes we have seen such illumination of spirit that the body becomes redundant in a conscious dying of infinite beauty. Meditation seems to open the door in this life and beyond . . .

Most of us cannot learn easily without the help of a teacher and guide. If you are reading this, then it is probably true for you that "the pupil is ready; the teacher comes". I have already mentioned that I have made many abortive attempts to travel the road of meditation until I met Jessica Macbeth, and I am enormously grateful to her that she has collected her teaching notes into this excellent book.

You will find the many ideas and instructions so elegantly and humorously expressed here that it is simplicity itself to follow. And never for a moment will you feel that these are words dropping graciously from the lips of a guru! Much more, you will have a sense of being with a rugged fellow-traveller who knows the road just a bit better than you and, pointing to the signposts, helps you to have fun while you journey together.

Moon over Water guides us across the Plain of Reflections, calms the emotional waters of the Sea of Changes and leads us up the mountain path to the Place of Light. We may meet with difficulties: dragons and serpents, thunder and lightning, trackless forests and fogs of confusion. We may indeed feel ourselves adrift on a stormy sea, but like all good pilgrims, we know that our daily practice is simply a path leading to the Place of Light where "all is One".

Moon over Water is going to be my constant companion as I journey - — I hope it will be yours too.

Pat Pilkington
Co-founder of the Bristol Cancer Help Centre

Bristol October 1989

Please note the Jessica Macbeth has recorded a number of tapes to go with this and her later books. Please turn to p. 181 for details.

Acknowledgements

With gratitude ...

to Don Holland for inspiration, for time and thought, for patience about reading stuff he already knew over and over, for telling me when I said it wrong, for helping me to get it right, and for friendship;

to Leona Williams Berger, for first teaching me to meditate (and much else) and for insisting that I do it;

to Sammye Souder for encouragement and beginnings;

to John Logan for much information, years of generous support, and Breathing In Truth, Breathing Out Not-Truth;

to Judy Dean for loving wisdom and grace and guidance — and much else;

to Judith Bromley for a magical encounter among standing stones and for artistic inspiration and encouragement;

to Nancy Nelson for friendship, awareness, and sharing;

to Elizabeth St. John for knowledge and generous teaching and being an old friend in a new land;

to Alick Bartholomew for being a friend, and for having faith, explaining things, seeing it through, and making it all possible;

to Sonja Clement for knowing the difference and for enthusiasm;

to Pat Pilkington for making connections and giving loving support;

to Jenny Jackson for 'trial reading', for being her delightful self, and for letting me watch her grow;

to Dee Schwartz Logan for suggestions and for doing the cooking as deadlines drew ever nearer;

to Warren Wise for the computer, without which this probably would never have happened;

to the members of the Order of the Ascending Spirit for sharing the path in kindness and love;

to all the people in the Wednesday Groups — especially Joe Bibbey, Felicity Bowers, Wanda Butler, Don Holland, Gemma Ireland, Jonathan Lane, Olga Lawrence, Nancy Nelson, Su O'Donnell, Bonnie Proctor, Indre Ratiu, Ian Roberts, Celia Thomas, Tamara Ward Vogel, Columb Whelan, and Warren Wise — and to June Hall-Hall and Sam Butler, who are gone but not to be forgotten; and

to all the many, many others, especially my students, who have so generously shared their wisdom and taught and guided me over the years.

Introduction

This is a guide book to the fascinating world of meditation as I have learned to know it since I first began meditating about twenty years ago. I'd always been interested in our potential mental abilities and capacities, but until then, hadn't encountered anyone who could teach me much about the things that aroused my curiosity. Then my aunt learned to meditate. She felt that she was getting so much out of it that she suggested (pretty forcefully) that I do it too, and taught me a very basic meditation exercise. I practised it and found it a terrible struggle, but also discovered almost immediate rewards.

So here we are about twenty years later, with many books read, some teachers listened to, and hours and hours and hours of practice. Obviously, I find something worth while about this process. In fact, it would not be an exaggeration to say that it has changed my life. The first changes I noticed were physical — my allergies faded away to nothing, my low blood pressure normalised, my blood sugar became much more balanced, and a long-standing tendency to colds and chest complaints virtually disappeared. I didn't have anything desperately wrong with me — just the sort of thing most of us accumulate in time — but it was pleasing to see these things just fade away. And there was more. I found that I was calmer, and that because I was calmer, I was better able to cope with the various stresses of my life. Things didn't rock me off my balance so easily. Again, nothing extreme, but it was valuable to me. And there was still more. My spiritual life opened up like a flower in the springtime.

In addition to meditating during the past twenty years, I have also taught many other people to meditate, either as an end in itself or as part of a self-development programme. In fact, this book had its beginning in notes and exercises for my classes. Anyone who has used a word processor knows how easy it is to change a little here and add a bit there. My notes kept growing and growing over the years just to provide the 'essential' information my students seemed to need. Finally, they (the notes, not the students) became unmanageable and began to look like an embryo book.

I suggested the book to Alick Bartholomew of Gateway Books, and he liked the idea of a concise guide to meditation. We both felt there was a need for an up-to-date book which clearly and simply set forth the what, why, and how of meditation. There seemed to be a place for a book which would discuss the process of meditation itself, explaining some of its possibilities and offering a variety of techniques, but leaving it to you to choose just what you want to do with it. You might say that we wanted to create a map that showed the territory and let you decide just where you want to go, and which path you want to take to get there.

I hope that your journey through this inner land will be rich and rewarding.

Part I

On the Nature of the Territory

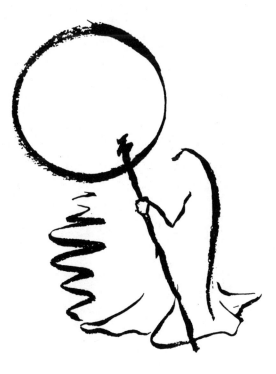

1. What We May Find

When we first begin to practise meditation, we discover a whole new world in ourselves. In some ways we are already familiar with this world, but it also contains gifts, treasures, skills, talents, and other things we may never have suspected. Exploring this inner world is one of the most exciting and useful things we can ever do. The practice of meditation takes us on a journey of growth and discovery — growth into what we have the creative potential of becoming, and discovery of strengths and magic in ourselves that we never knew we had.

As we begin to investigate this inner world, it may help to visualise it in a symbolic form. Imagine, if you will, a vast plain, the Plain of Reflections, the inner world of the mind. Upon this plain, there are great universities and libraries filled with wisdom and knowledge. Well-equipped laboratories exist where we can discover and learn even more. There is even an ivory tower, from which we may explore, built upon the border of the unknown lands.

There are forests in which we may become lost and confused, or be frightened by beasts, both mythical and real. There are deserts where we feel isolated and lonely, and deep canyons into which we may fall, with mental dragons lurking in the bottom. These canyons divide the Plain of Reflections into hundreds of small kingdoms, many isolated from the others. In these kingdoms, people are doing all of the things people do — exciting and dull, honest and dishonest, creative and destructive. Some of these people wear the masks of people we know, but underneath they all have our own secret face.

The Plain of Reflections has much rich soil, and great growth can take place in this inner world of the mind. There are hidden treasures to find, and unknown paths upon which we may seek adventure. We could spend our entire lives exploring the Plain of Reflections, our own mental resources and awareness — and our time would not have been wasted. But there is more to our inner world than this.

In the centre of this plain, imagine a large body of water — so large that it really must be called an inland sea. It is the waters of emotion, the Sea of Changes. It is quite a magical sea, capable of being as salt and bitter as tears one moment, violently stormy another, or clear and sparkling with waves prancing joyously in the sunlight. Ancient creatures from the dawn of time live in its depths, and during storms they rise to the surface to frighten the unwary.

Storms sometimes rage from the sea out over the land, wreaking devastation where they pass — or mists may arise from the waters, drawn up by the sun, and fall as gentle rain which nourishes all that grows upon the plain. The condition of this sea governs the weather of the entire inner world. Sometimes a deep calm falls upon the Sea of Changes. Upon the still water every star is clearly reflected, and in that peace the unbearably sweet song of mermaids rises to the heavens.

In the centre of the Sea of Changes there rises a steep-sided mountain, the impregnable and unexplored core of our being. This, for most of us, is truly *terra incognita*, the unknown land. From the far shore of the Plain of Reflections, the mountain appears difficult of access, impossible to climb. Its head is hidden in the clouds of heaven and its roots run deeply into the heart of the earth.

When the water of the sea is rough, the mountain is completely cut off from the plain. When the sea is smoother, we can venture close enough to see that it might well be possible, in a complete calm, to land on the mountain and to begin to ascend its precipitous side toward the hidden crest. Such calms are quite rare, and when we are climbing the mountain, the sea must remain calm — the slightest disturbance on its surface will splash up the mountainside, causing us to lose our footing and come tumbling back down into the water.

But there is another way, a magical way, up the mountain at the centre of being. Everyone, everything we meet in this land is an image, another face of ourselves — people, dragons, mirages, chasms, mountains, towers, weather, grass, paths, obstacles, mountains. Everything is our own secret face reflected back to us. Imagine that each of these images has a bell that it is ringing. Some are chiming gently, some loudly, some discordantly clanging, some mellow and harmonious. You have given yourself the task of bringing all these bells into tune, as you travel through this world, so they will sing out in a single, bright, plangent note.

When this happens, when there are no discords, when your entire being joins into one, the note shifts and rises beyond our normal hearing range, into an intense and full silence. In that moment, the plain becomes quiet, the sea utterly still, the clouds part, and we see the moon riding high in the sky over the mountain. At such a time, we, standing on the silent shore, see a smooth path of light shining over the water, an illumination of the spirit, leading right up to the unknown crest of the mountain. If we venture upon the path, we are borne swiftly and effortlessly to the Place of Light at the summit. From here we can see the entire Plain of Reflections, the Sea of Changes, the stars of the heavens, and the depths beyond. In such a moment we feel the roots of the mountain in the earth, the song of the stars, and we know ourselves to be one with the whole.

Meditation is one way to journey through this inner world, to discover its real nature and strengths, and to tune the bells to the one note that changes this world. As a first step on this journey, let's try a simple exercise.

First, make certain that no one will interrupt you for the next five minutes. Then, sit in a comfortable position, shut your eyes, and be aware of your breath. Feel it coming in, feel it going out. Feel your chest and abdomen moving as you breathe. Don't pay attention to anything except your breath. Completely ignore any sounds you hear, any thoughts that come into your mind, any other bodily sensations or feelings. Give your breath your complete and undivided attention for five minutes.

Did you have any problems doing this? Did uninvited thoughts go racing through your mind? Were you at all distracted by the sounds or other things in your environment? Did your breathing become muddled because you were paying attention to it? Were you surprised by how difficult it was to hold your concentration for so short a time as five minutes? Were you surprised at how very long five minutes can actually be? Did you have any feelings of surprise, frustration or anger at the recalcitrance and lack of discipline of your mind? Did you have any feelings of discomfort about being still for that long?

The question that everyone asks is, 'Why meditate?' Why sit there for fifteen minutes every day, doing nothing? Isn't it, some say, just an excuse to be self-indulgent and idle? Only someone who has never tried a simple meditation technique, like the exercise above, could suggest such a thing. It is, especially in the beginning, one of the most difficult things most of us ever try to do. However, there are several good reasons for doing it.

The practice of meditation can reduce tension and promote relaxation, improve concentration and self-discipline, give a sense of improved well-being, increase energy, aid the development of the psyche, enhance spiritual growth, lower high blood pressure, decrease the frequency and severity of tension-related diseases, aid the body in its recovery from physical fatigue (in some ways faster than sleep), promote serenity, and improve your ability to listen (to others, to your body, and to yourself). These are only a part of the practical benefits, and in addition to them, meditation is free, non-toxic, non-fattening, and it has no artificial additives or colourings. What more could we ask in exchange for a bit of our time and awareness?

Yet, there is more — meditation is something we do for ourselves, a gift from ourselves to ourselves. Through it we discover the land within — the exciting, fascinating, rich plain of the mind, the vast deep sea of the emotions, and the mountain in the centre, the strong core of ourselves, rooted in the earth and reaching to the heavens. We discover what lies beyond the superficial surface, and we see who we really are. We often speak of needing to love and value ourselves, to have true self-esteem and a sense of self-worth, but we seldom seem to have much idea of how to do this. Meditation is a loving gift we can give ourselves that helps us to build a positive attitude toward our own being and to discover the light within us.

People are learning much more about the relationship between the mind and the body. Increasingly, we are coming to understand that what we think affects our feelings, and both our thoughts and our feelings affect our health. And yet, the part of ourselves over which we seem to have the least control is our thoughts. We are frequently lost in the overgrown woods and cannot see the forest for the trees. Meditation is a way of learning to exercise some control over what goes on in our heads.

It is easy for most of us to understand why the athlete does stretches and muscle-building exercises in addition to his sport — the whole body needs to be strong, flexible, and working in harmony in order to do a specific activity well. The musician is taught scales and exercises that develop dexterity, fluency, strength, control, and awareness. So, too, the artist, practising exercises that increase manual dexterity and control, enhances her ability to really see accurately, and to transmit what comes in the eye to canvas or clay. If you can't draw a vase accurately, you can't draw an image in your mind accurately either.

Talent alone is never enough — skill and technique are required if we are going to develop and use a talent, and we can only acquire these things through practice. If we want to develop the potential strength, clarity, awareness, flexibility, and control of our minds, there are also exercises to help us — exercises that have been known and practised in virtually all cultures for many thousands of years.

All of the meditation exercises to be described later share certain results, the treasures to be found in this inner world. These results (or more accurately, 'side-effects') of meditation fall into three basic categories: practical and physical, psychological, and spiritual. We will consider the psychological and spiritual effects later on, but first let's look at the practical and physical effects.

2. Treasures Found by the Wayside

Almost as soon as we begin our inner journey, we find treasures by the wayside — practical, down-to-earth benefits that happen just because we are meditating. Some of these were mentioned briefly above, but let's take a closer look at how our practice gives us these things.

Concentration & Self-Discipline

The ability to concentrate, to keep our attention on one thing, without distraction, so that we can bring our full mental capacity to bear upon it, is a skill. Like other skills, concentration can be improved with practice. Meditation *is* concentration, a special kind of relaxed but focused awareness. It is concentration without strain.

Many of us have been conditioned to the idea that concentration must involve strain and tension in order to be effective. This is part of the world-view that says that anything worth while must be difficult — and therefore, this view illogically goes on to conclude, anything easy must be worthless. This seems to mean that we must tense up our neck, shoulder and facial muscles in order to think well. If we scrunched over our desks, clutching our pencil so hard that our little knuckles turned white, the teacher knew we were *trying*.

The problem with this, of course, is that our energy and attention went into trying (and into being seen to be trying) rather than into thinking. It seems fairly obvious that our brains must function better when oxygen and nutrients reach them freely than they do when the blood supply is cut down by muscular tension. But then how would we (and others) know that we were really trying? On the face of it this attitude may seem silly, but most of us developed it when we were quite young and are still deeply influenced by it. Have you ever noticed that *attention* sounds just like *at tension?*

Meditation gives us a chance to let go of the habit of struggling to focus our awareness, and it allows us to practise concentration combined with deep relaxation. As we get better at letting go in meditation, we begin to discover how much more effectively we can concentrate when we put less effort into other things — things like pressing our lips tightly together and frowning. We tend to carry this new way of being into other aspects of our lives.

This means we have more energy for actual thinking and we tend to do it more clearly and efficiently. Although there are a few people who seem to get by without using their minds much, most of us would find an improved ability to concentrate and to ignore distraction to be an advantage in many aspects of life. A person who has reached an advanced stage of this relaxed concentration may even be able to do her accounts without moving her shoulders closer to her ears.

The word concentrate is derived from words meaning *to join in one centre*, and meditation is about bringing ourselves to the peaceful centre of our own beings, the mountain in the centre of the sea. From that peaceful centre, we can think and act with balance and grace, rather than with stress and confusion.

Self-discipline is closely related to concentration. Most of us, in order to carry out a regular programme of meditation, need to be more self-disciplined than we usually are. No one makes us do it; perhaps no one even cares whether we do it or not. It is entirely up to us. Our best reason for doing it is *for ourselves*. We are the ones who benefit, and the benefits may or may not be noticed much by others.

There is a potential self-sustaining positive feedback loop here. Doing our meditation exercises regularly is a way of exercising our self-discipline. When we do anything often, we tend to become better at it. In this case, the better we are at it, the more practice we get. Like the strengthening of concentration in meditation, the exercise of self-discipline spills over into our daily life, encouraging us to be that bit more disciplined, organised, and efficient in other ways — which in turn helps us to be more disciplined about our meditation practice. Round and round we go, gaining on each turn.

Relaxation & Self-Healing

The ability to reduce habitual or excessive tension is achieved easily and naturally through meditation. Deep relaxation often occurs in meditation, and is, in fact, an indication that we are meditating well. When we are deeply relaxed in meditation, amazing things can happen in our bodies. These are achieved much more effectively and rapidly through meditation than through the ordinary relaxation which usually occurs when we sit back and let go of our attention.

For example, tests[1] have shown that the amount of blood lactate (which increases rapidly during stress or anxiety) is reduced substantially more quickly during meditation than during sleep or ordinary relaxation. Many people find it surprising that such simple *mental* exercises can have a significant and measurable physiological effect, but there is even more. Other physiological indicators of tension such as heartbeat rate, blood pressure, and oxygen consumption are also beneficially affected. Additionally, some of the stress-related diseases, especially high blood pressure and tension headaches, may be alleviated — or even eliminated — by regular meditation.

These physiological effects alone would justify the practice of meditation even if there were no other benefits to be obtained from it. Tension-related diseases are by far the most common disorders in our society. These diseases are apt to be either chronic or recurring and are often not very responsive to the usual medical treatments.

When we practise consistently we find that we not only become unusually relaxed during the meditation period itself, but also that our reactions to tension and stressful situations in everyday life gradually change. Over a period of time we develop a calmer, more relaxed, and probably more constructive response.

We all know that we are more apt to catch an illness if we are tired or stressed. To be more relaxed and generally less stressed enhances our resistance to contagious disease[2]. And if we do get ill, meditation and its accompanying deep relaxation enables the natural repair systems of our bodies to function more effectively. This is only reasonable — energy being used to maintain a state of tension or stress is not available to the organism to use for self-healing. When we free that energy for healing ourselves, we naturally speed the healing process.

Listening

Perhaps the most difficult and yet one of the most important of the things that we may expect to learn from the continued practice of meditation is the ability to really listen — to be silent within our own minds, so that we can hear as we probably have not heard since childhood. This kind of listening can be directed inwardly as well as outwardly. Relaxation and improved concentration occur simply because meditation is practised, but learning to listen well does require additional effort.

Everyone realises from their own experience that people often do not really listen to what others are saying. During any conversation, while one person is speaking, the other is usually 'listening', making evaluations about what is being said, and formulating a reply — all simultaneously. We cannot hear clearly because we are listening to the the other person speak and at the same time talking to ourselves — and usually paying more attention to our own voice inside our heads.

All too often the listener doesn't actually hear much of the other person's thoughts at all. He simply assumes that the speaker is going to say certain things, and his evaluation and reply are based on this assumption rather than on what is actually being said. This may be good enough for a lot of casual exchanges, but conversations of greater depth and importance deserve better listening. This principle also applies to inner-directed listening or awareness, where we learn about ourselves and clarify our own needs and feelings. Our Plain of Reflections needs to be still, listening, aware.

Self-Awareness

How many of us are truly aware of the things our bodies are trying to tell us? Do we always notice the warning signals such as excessive fatigue, irritability, mild depression, lowered levels of physical, psychological, and/or psychic energy, little aches and pains, increased tension, and so on? These are some of the signals which come before a malfunction or breakdown of the physical or mental processes. Any change in our physical or emotional health is always heralded by such warnings, but often we are too distracted or too unaware to notice them. We usually travel through life so dazzled by the outer world that we are only aware of the inner when it goes seriously amiss.

Meditation helps us to become more aware of these signals. It gives us practice in monitoring the subtle changes that take place within ourselves, not only physically, but also mentally, emotionally, and energetically. As we become more aware of ourselves, we learn to correlate various physical and emotional states and to recognise more clearly than ever before how feelings affect our physical and mental states. Too many people, when asked how they *feel*, say what they are *thinking* and cannot give a clear answer about their actual feelings. When we meditate, we gradually become much more self-aware and in touch with our feelings and bodies. We not only know how to relax, but also to recognise more readily when we need to let go.

Sensitivity

At first, as we practise meditation, we begin to sense the subtle changes in physical, mental, and emotional states in ourselves. Later on, we usually begin to be more aware of these subtle energies in others as well. We become more aware of these energies and states, whether they come from our physical bodies, our unconscious minds, or the bodies and minds of others. In fact, one could say that our awareness expands to include areas of our own minds that were previously unconscious.

One of the important functions of meditation exercises is to teach the verbal and analysing part of the mind to be quiet so that the more subtle, non-verbal signals are able to get through more often and more clearly. Because we have greater clarity about these personal warnings of stress and fatigue, and because we have increased sensitivity to and understanding of the needs of ourselves and others, we also develop an increased sense of 'rightness' or 'wrongness' in situations requiring choice. This makes our 'hunches' and 'intuition' both more clear and more accurate.

These are results that most meditation exercises have in common. They are the natural consequences of doing these kinds of exercises, but many, probably even most of these exercises were originally developed for another purpose.

3. Treasures of the Psyche and Spirit

There are other, more subtle treasures that we find as we go — joys of the psyche and spirit. These are like rare butterflies and brilliant sunrises, joys of the moment which may have a lasting effect upon us. Once upon a time long, long ago, practically everything was 'spiritual'. Early people saw everything as being alive, and they saw everything, including themselves, as being divine. By trial and error over the millennia they developed a number of techniques for experiencing a quality in themselves and in the world which they believed to be the presence of divinity. Among these techniques are many of those that we presently practise as meditation exercises.

Those ancient people might not have considered most of the things we have discussed as especially important — they probably took many of them for granted. They lived a different lifestyle, were more in tune with nature, handled stress differently, and probably took for granted a number of the attitudes and experiences that we have to work at today in our industrial, crowded, hurried culture. For them, contact with nature and with a sense of a higher power of some sort was an integrated and inextricable part of everyday life. My first reason for believing this is that they *did* develop the exercises which have come down through the centuries. My second (and, I think, more important) reason is that many children spontaneously have these magical, mystical experiences of a numinous quality in the world and in themselves — until they learn to think and function in a way that inhibits those perceptions.

These contacts, when refined and clarified, may lead to the experience we now call the 'mystical experience' or *'satori'* or *'kensho'* or *'nirvana'* or 'bliss' or any of several other names. It was discovered long ago that the practice of certain specialised mental (and sometimes physical) exercises lead to these experiences. Those techniques have been handed down for generation after generation wherever such experiences and the inner growth they evoke are valued.

Here the road splits, with some heading up the ecstasy-for-its-own-sake dead end, while others continue on and use the ecstatic experience as an illumination of the shadows within themselves and a driving force for personal and spiritual growth. It is because the experience of ecstasy and the resultant psychological and spiritual growth were originally the primary purposes in meditation and are still that for many people, that I have called the things listed in the preceding pages 'side-effects', treasures found by the roadside.

In modern times we have separated the concepts of 'psyche' and 'spirit'. However, even in that separation, meditation increasingly is recognised today as a valuable aid in the personal growth process. It can help us to clear psychological blocks and to stabilise our emotional reactions, as well as giving us better insight into ourselves and others.

Now that we can begin to see some of the things we might gain from meditating, let's take a look at what meditation actually is.

4. Defining the Boundaries

One of the things that make our inner world so interesting to explore is that so much of the territory is marked *terra incognita* on the map. We know some of the places on the Plain of Reflections, we know the surface of the Sea of Changes, and many of us have at least glimpsed the mountain in the centre of the world. Much is yet unknown and unexplored. Before we embark upon our journey, let's consider where we may be going.

The word 'meditation' is like the word 'love' — it not only means different things to different people, but it also means different things to the same people at different times. If you ask ten people, you will get at least ten answers, perhaps even more. Some may say that it's thinking about a problem; some that it's sitting and watching the movies in your mind; some that it's practising particular types of exercises involving chants or complicated visualisations; some that it's chanting your *mantra* that is given to you by your *guru*; some that it's sitting quietly and waiting for inspiration; some that it's striving to achieve the inner silence; and some that it is the experience of union with God. The worst of it is, they're all right. Words are like people; they continue to grow and change as long as they live, and this word has a very long history.

Some Definitions & Differences

The words we use about things both determine and limit the way we think of them, so the first thing we must do if we really want to communicate clearly is to define our terms very carefully. Let's take a look at some of the dictionary definitions of *meditate* and a couple of related words:

Meditate *(Latin:* meditor = *to think, reflect upon, consider, design, propose, intend, exercise the mind, practise. Sanscrit:* madh-a = *wisdom.)* 1. *To reflect upon; to study, ponder.* 2. *To observe with intentness.* 3. *To plan by revolving in the mind; to design mentally.* 4. *To think.* 5. *To exercise the mind in thought or contemplation, especially devotional.*

Contemplation *(Latin:* con = *with, together — and* templum = *an open space for observation marked out by the augur.)* 1. *The action of beholding.* 2. *The action of mentally viewing; attentive consideration, study, meditation.* 3. *Religious reflection.*

Consider *(Latin:* con = *with, together — and* sidus *or* sideris = *the stars. To observe the stars.)* 1. *To view attentively, to survey, examine, inspect.* 2. *To look objectively.* 3. *To contemplate mentally, to think over, meditate on, give heed to, take note of.*

In common usage today, *meditate, consider,* and *contemplate* all mean much the same thing — to think about or reflect upon something. However, if we look at the origins of these words, some interesting concepts emerge. *Consider* has its roots in astrology, in seeing what the stars say about a question. *Contemplate* is derived from the reading of omens by an augur or soothsayer and the 'empty space' in which that reading was done. *Meditate* comes from the Sanskrit word for wisdom — which one may attain by logical thought, by understanding one's experiences, or by inspiration.

These words have passed through many different shades of meaning before reaching their present usage. At present, another layer is being added to the word *meditation*, which increasingly is being used to denote certain types of mental exercises aimed at achieving psychic and spiritual growth, increased mental and emotional stability, and improved physical health.

In this book we will be discussing the use of types of meditation exercises designed for a very specific purpose. These exercises are mental disciplines aimed at achieving a state of intently concentrated and yet relaxed stillness within ourselves — they are simply techniques for creating an inner silence, stilling the Plain of Reflections, calming the waters of the Sea of Changes. We shall borrow a concept from the word *contemplation* and say that we are trying to create an open space in the mind, which may allow the moon to create its magical path over the waters to the peak of the mountain.

The circle symbol used in the illustrations is called *enso* in Japanese. The Zen calligrapher uses it to symbolise the state of mystical union — "empty yet full, infinite, luminous, complete".[3] In the West, the circle has long been the sign of something that is endless, complete in itself, perfect. As used here, it is a symbol of that open space in the mind, the state of perfect stillness, as silent and reflective as the moon. Let us think for just a moment about what else might happen in this still, open space. Imagery and healing may happen or be evoked in the still and concentrated quiet. Images that occur or are deliberately called forth may be used to help us with self-exploration, self-healing, and relaxation; to gain insight; and to receive inspiration. Images may be visual, as people most often think of them, but they may also be auditory or kinesthetic — that is, we may see, hear, or feel them.

Insight, information, and inspiration may also come into the silent mind in other forms — as if we were remembering something we had once experienced or learned, or simply as a sudden thought, a burst of knowing. These things enter the busy-mind only with great difficulty, and then usually only when there is an interruption to its busy-ness and a momentary silence. This is yet another reason why these exercises, which teach the mind stillness and develop the openness necessary to self-awareness and psychic and spiritual growth, are so valuable.

It is important, however, to recognise that these things — insight, inspiration, healing — *are not meditation* as we are using the word here. They are something that may happen more strongly and clearly because we practise meditation and because we have trained our minds to be still and focused and to listen. Sometimes these things occur spontaneously during our meditation, and then they should be treated like any other distraction. If we wish, we may later use them for psychological or spiritual growth. True meditation, as we are defining it, is the practice of the exercises which create clarity and silence on the Plain of Reflections and calm and stillness on the Sea of Changes.

We have said a lot about what meditation is and what it does for us, but it may also be helpful to look briefly at some of the things it is not.

5. Here Be Dragons

It was the practice of ancient cartographers to mark unknown places with warnings like 'Abode of the Great Wyrm' or 'Here Lieth Monsters'. Although mapmakers nowadays are much less fanciful, we humans still come up with these interesting beliefs. There are a number of these ideas that people often put forth as reasons for not practising meditation. Usually these things are only said by people who have never practised — anyone who has knows better. We all know that *terra incognita* contains monsters — and the monsters are usually myths. If you tell many people that you have begun practising, you may well hear some of these comments from a few of them.

It would be selfish and self-indulgent to waste all that time on myself. Two important things are wrong with this. First, it implies that the speaker is not worth or entitled to the ten or twenty minutes a day needed to meditate. This seems to indicate a distressingly poor sense of self-esteem. Secondly, it also assumes that all of the things that meditation does for us do not, in turn, affect the way we deal with other people. This is obviously untrue. In fact, many people, when they first begin to practise, receive positive comments from others before they notice any changes in themselves. Others are often very quick to notice that we have become calmer, more sensitive, more objective, and more aware — and they are usually relieved and pleased that this is happening.

Of course, when someone else gives this excuse to you, part of what they may be saying is that *you* are selfish and self-indulgent to be spending time on yourself — especially if you might otherwise be spending it on the speaker.

Meditation is addictive. People who do it say they feel worse when they don't do it, so this means it is an addiction. Meditation fulfils a need of the mind and spirit just as food and exercise fulfil needs of the body. People who have a well-balanced physical exercise programme nearly always say that they feel worse when they don't do their exercises. This is because the body knows what is good for it and misses it when it is not there. The practice of meditation is much the same. An addiction, on the other hand, is usually something that gives us a short-term 'high' of some sort and long-term damage.

In actual fact, there is something interesting going on here. When we begin meditating, we feel better. After a while we begin to accept the new feeling as 'normal' and forget that we once habitually felt less alive, less energetic, less peaceful. Then, if we skip our practice for a day or two and again start to feel as we formerly felt all of the time, we think we feel badly — although, by any objective measure, we may still feel more peaceful and healthier than we once considered 'normal'. Humans are like that.

If I need to calm myself, I don't need to meditate. All I need to do is think about it and control myself that way. There is a difference between emotional suppression (which is what that kind of 'self-control' is usually about) and letting go. The suppression of our feelings leaves us with an underlayer of emotion, covered by a layer of rigidity, like a disturbed sea with swift currents, covered by a layer of ice. This is harmful to our health, as the cigarette advertisements say. In meditation, we let go. Instead of forcing ourselves into calmness, we relax into it, and we help ourselves to develop a habit of calmness. We learn to be calm when there is no reason for anxiety, instead of maintaining a level of arousal that is not called for by our present circumstances 'just in case' we might need it.

I don't need to meditate — my problems are purely physical (or my problems are real). Akin to this is: *My doctor prescribed meditation, but I really need new pills.* This supposes that the mind does not affect the body, and that the body does not affect the mind. Neither of these things seem to be true

When we are hungry (or too full) or tired or ill, we all know that we do not think as quickly or as clearly as we do when we feel well-balanced physically. It is also being recognised by increasing numbers of people that the mind very much affects the body. Meditation is currently being prescribed by some up-to-date doctors and therapists for things like high blood pressure, certain heart conditions, migraine headaches, cancer, and other stress-related illnesses. Unlike many of the medications and treatments prescribed for such illnesses, meditation has no harmful side-effects.

*I meditate when I go out for a walk (*or *when I run* or *when I practise Yoga* or *T'ai Chi). I don't need to sit down and do it.* Only someone who doesn't understand what meditation is and what complete stillness does for us could say this. How can you be absolutely still, with your body very relaxed and your mind alert, when you are walking or running or doing any kind of exercise? Once you have read the exercises in the next chapter, you will see that it would be very difficult to meditate with full attention on the process while going for a walk.

It is, of course, possible to walk, run, or exercise in a calm and meditative state of mind, and this is very useful as a part of a programme of reducing stress and developing a more serene attitude toward life. However, it is not a substitute for sitting meditation. There are even some moving meditations, but they are considered to be supplements to rather than replacements for sitting.

Meditation? Isn't that something those swamis in funny robes do? And along with this is: *Meditation is something that weirdos do, it isn't for ordinary people.* It is true that some very strange and unusual people practise meditation techniques. It is also true that most swamis meditate. So do many dervishes, yogis, monks, nuns, pop stars, actors, plumbers, computer programmers, shamans, housewives, business executives, policemen, models, salespersons, writers, and others. Einstein is quoted as having said that an idea is not responsible for the people who believe in it. Meditation is not responsible for the people who practise it.

And what, pray tell, is an 'ordinary person'? The general definition seems to be either 'someone just like me' or 'one of the common people who are unlike thou and I, superior people that we are'. Neither definition seems very useful to me.

Meditation takes you out of the real world, and you lose touch with reality. Here is one with just a tiny touch of pseudo-truth about it. A very few (but alas, very conspicuous) people do use 'meditation' and 'spirituality' as an excuse for an escape from reality. This only works if what they are really doing is 'spacing out' rather than actual disciplined meditation exercises. If we are practising properly, it helps us to be more in touch with reality rather than less — think about the things we talked about earlier.

Everything about life can be seen as a spiritual exercise. This means that getting our work done, keeping the house clean, paying the bills, honouring our obligations to ourselves and others, being of service, experiencing joy and pain and all the rest of it are a part of our *spiritual* exercise. Everyday life is not separate from spirituality, and people who use their 'spiritual growth' as an excuse to avoid responsibility are actually hindering their spiritual development. The kind of person who is avoiding reality may use something that they call 'meditation' to help them do so, but they are unlikely to be using any of the simple but rather demanding techniques described in this book. If you are not already looking for an escape route from real life, you are most unlikely to use your meditation practice in that way.

Meditation, because it helps us to do a lot of very practical things, is a useful tool. Like all tools — think of all the things you can do with a hammer — we can use it constructively or destructively. As we saw in the last chapter, many of the side-effects of meditation (increased concentration, reduced stress, better self-discipline, and others) are obviously very useful — in fact, they are so useful that many people meditate just for those practical effects and not for any 'spiritual' reason at all.

Meditation creates a hypnotic state, and we may not be able to come back from it. This is pure superstition. First, a fact about hypnosis: if you go into a hypnotic trance and no one wakes you up, you fall into a normal sleep and waken when you are rested[4]. This is something that is known and understood by those who have studied hypnosis. Secondly, meditation is not hypnosis. They are both altered states of consciousness, but so are sleep and daydreaming — and no one suggests that they are hypnosis. Very few people even believe that they are dangerous. This particular statement reflects not only ignorance about what meditation is, but also a lack of knowledge about hypnosis.

Meditation can release forces we don't understand, and they can be dangerous. More superstition, and closely related to the one above. Many people are afraid of the mysterious powers of their own minds. They believe that a human's hold on sanity is fragile. This leads us — when we remember that people often project onto others what they fear in themselves — to feel concern for *their* hold on sanity. It is true that our minds are wonderful instruments, capable of doing really astonishing things — and that some of these things can be most unpleasant, even frightening. However, meditation contributes to stability rather than instability, to health rather than to illness.

Meditation is the work of the Devil. If someone says this to you, there is no point in trying to argue with them. There is no reasoning with that kind of statement — it is an article of faith. It is not based on logic; it is probably based on fear. People who say this sort of thing usually don't know anything about meditation, nor do they want to. They have rigid rules to live by and believe that any deviation from those rules will cause God to cast them out and the Devil will get them.

What we need to realise is that such a response is a-rational — it is outside of reason. Anyone who tries to change another's a-rational view by the use of logic might as well be speaking Sanskrit to a brick. However, it does bring us to the interesting subject of religion and meditation.

Meditation is only for religious people, and I'm not religious. One of the common misunderstandings about meditation is the belief that it is 'only' a religious exercise. It *is* practised by some of the followers of nearly all religions, but is not, in its basic form, a religious activity. In fact, as we have mentioned, it is now being practised by many business people who are not religious, but who have learned of the practical value of mental exercises which promote improved health, clearer thinking, and a less stressed attitude toward life.

One of the reasons for this confusion is that, in traditional Christian terms, meditation is often an actual specialised kind of 'thinking about' a particular aspect of religion. In that tradition, the type of exercises that are now generally referred to as meditation were once a part of contemplative practice, and were not called meditation at all. Somehow, in the movement of Eastern (especially Indian) exercises to Europe and America, the words became used differently and even greater confusion ensued.

As you will see, meditation techniques are simple exercises, which happen to have complex and beneficial effects on the body and the emotional state, but the techniques themselves haven't anything to do with religion or faith. So we see that these exercises are not 'religious' in the sense that they are a part of any one religion and not of others, but they are certainly spiritual, as every aspect of life is. Daily life is a spiritual exercise, no one part of it more than another, and in that context these techniques are spiritual exercises. They are also physical, emotional, and mental exercises as well. They exercise body, mind, and spirit.

6. The Heart of the Land

So what is this journey really about? If we are travelling the path of meditation, where can we expect to go? Meditation is the practice of specific techniques or exercises for creating a still and open space in our beings. We can learn and practise these techniques, learning to quiet the activities on the Plain of Reflections and to still the Sea of Changes. There is, however, more to it than this. Our self-created open space, *of its own accord*, fills with relaxation, serenity, and vitality. We become like a still, deep sea, filled with the numinous white light of the moon. When we become calm and at peace with ourselves and the moon casts its path across the waters to the shore, something quite magical and indescribable may happen.

For thousands of years poets and saints and artists and mystics have tried to describe this experience. They all agree that nothing else is like it, they all agree that it changes the one who experiences it, they all agree that it is one of — indeed, usually *the* most important thing that has happened to them, and they all agree that it is the experience of some sort of union — though with what or with whom they are less in agreement. The mystical experience is universal and found in every time and culture. The descriptions of it are based on various cultural belief systems and religions.

Sometimes people meditate for years without having a mystical experience. Others may have the experience even without meditation, although it is generally agreed that meditation makes us more open to such an experience. There are no guarantees.

There are two things to remember. First, while you may or may not ever have a mystical experience, meditation has much to offer you, enriching all aspects of your life, both practical and spiritual. Second, the mystical experience, blissful as it is, is a beginning, not an end. When it does happen, it empowers a process of change that continues for years and requires our on-going attention and work and growth.

Now that we have looked at what meditation is and is not, let's look as what is involved in its actual practice.

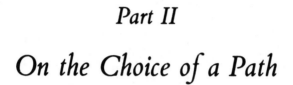

Part II

On the Choice of a Path

7. Exploring New Lands

In exploring new places, it helps to have some idea of the terrain, what we will find there, and its likely affect upon us. As you will see, there are quite a variety of basic meditation techniques. Your own personality and needs will determine which path you choose for your own practice. For example, some of the exercises require the visualisation of something as the focal point of concentration. If you have difficulty in visualising, it is obviously going to be easier for you to begin with one of the exercises that does not require this.

In considering which technique is best for you, there are several factors to take into consideration. In the following chapters some of the more important differences are discussed, and example exercises are given in each chapter.

Some of the exercises have a comment recommending some kind of previous experience. If there is no such comment, the exercise is considered a good one for complete novices, as well as for those with experience.

More complete information about actual practice will be given later, but here are a few brief suggestions to help you get started.

If possible, meditation should be done while sitting erect in a firm chair — or on the floor cross-legged if your body likes that. Your back should be erect, but not tense or rigid. The spine should rest into its natural curves, but it is important not to collapse or slump.

Organise things beforehand so that you will have the least possible number of interruptions. Disconnect the phone.

Practise the exercise for ten minutes.

As you read through the information below, don't worry about getting it exactly right the first time. It will all become more clear as you progress through this guide book.

8. Inner or Outer?

The first choice we need to make is to choose between are the inner focus and outer focus techniques. The inner focus exercises, frequently used in Yoga, involve using something within the self — usually the breath or an inner sound or image — as the core of the exercise. The outer focus techniques, often found in Zen Buddhist exercises, involve using something outside the self, often simultaneously with something inside the self — for example, looking at a candle while attending to the breath.

These two types of exercise produce slightly different brainwave patterns and a slightly different response to the world is encouraged. An experiment was done which compared brainwaves generated by the Yoga and Zen techniques and the meditator's response to a sudden noise. The Yogi reacted to the first sound by losing his concentration and taking a little while to get it back. When the sound was repeated, he lost his concentration less each time and took a shorter time to regain his one-pointedness, until after a couple of repetitions he didn't respond to the sound at all. On the other hand, the Roshi, a Zen master, responded distinctly to the sound, but immediately regained his focus. Each time the sound was repeated, his response was the same, hearing and letting go almost instantly.

This reflects a basic philosophical difference between the two ways of thinking. Yoga exercises are about self-control and tend to focus within ourselves, separate from the world, sometimes even separate from our own bodies. They encourage blocking out sensory experience. Zazen, a type of Zen Buddhist meditation, encourages a special meditative kind of awareness in the world and a readiness to respond to situations without emotional reaction and with the capacity to dismiss the experience immediately, if that is appropriate.

Many people find the inner focus techniques, which are usually done with the eyes shut, less difficult in the beginning. Having the eyes shut reduces the number of distractions available to the mind. However, some people find it easier to practise with their eyes slightly open and their gaze lowered. One of the indications of which type of exercise might be best for you is your general level of sensitivity and distractability. Those who are easily influenced by the thoughts and feelings of others may find that practising with open eyes is of special value. Open-eyed exercises tend to affect our brainwaves in ways that seem to enhance a certain kind of mental centeredness. This, in turn, helps us to be more focused and less influenced by our environment. This, like the other side-effects of meditation, tends to carry over into daily life.

If you have been using an inner focus technique for some length of time already, you might want to try one of the outer focus ones as a way of expanding your skills.

Inner Focus

1. Sit. Relax. Think of a simple design such as a circle around a cross or some other easily visualised symbol. Visualise this during your entire practice period, but do not try to think about what it symbolises in any way.

The design should be kept simple. It should not be complicated, unbalanced, or scattered. Preferably it should be within a circular form and should have a well-defined centre. Use the same design each time.

Because the inner focus exercises are entirely within ourselves, we can practise them anywhere and under any circumstances. One of the considerations in choosing an outer focus is how much of a problem this will cause in practising regularly. Some outer foci, such as your thumbnail or a blank wall, are fairly available, but others could be a problem.

Outer Focus

2. Sit. Relax. Rest your hand in front of you so that you can look down at your thumbnail with your eyelids lowered. Look intently at your thumbnail, but without straining your eyes. Keep your eyes and eyelids relaxed.

Be aware of the movement of your breath in your abdomen. During the entire exercise, stay aware of your breath, and keep observing your thumbnail. Do not think about your thumbnail or try to be profound about it — just look at it attentively, as if it were the most interesting thing you have ever seen.

9. Passive or Active?

Another way of categorising the techniques is into passive and active types. In a passive exercise we simply let our minds wander on their own, without any conscious direction on our part. We observe our thoughts without doing anything with them. This is far more difficult than it may sound. The temptation to follow up a spontaneous thought, actively thinking about and analysing it, is very nearly irresistible. However, a few people do find this the easiest technique with which to begin.

The active exercises are usually easiest for most people in the beginning. Many different techniques fall into this category. In this type of exercises we choose (or, in some kinds of training, have chosen for us) something upon which to focus our concentration.

There are two apparent sources for disruptions and distractions in our minds (although I suspect that there is really only one source and it has two techniques). One thing that happens is that the unconscious sends up a thought-bubble just about every ninety seconds. Often we don't notice these thought-bubbles because our minds are occupied with something else. When our minds are less busy, we may use these bubbles as the seeds for daydreams or build elaborate thought-castles around them. However, when we are trying to practise, they seem very disruptive and are often glaringly visible. In fact, they sometimes seem to come equipped with flashing neon lights and sirens.

In the passive type of exercise, we simply watch the thought-bubbles without becoming involved with them. In the active techniques, we (try to) ignore them, keeping our awareness on the chosen focus of the exercise.

In addition to this internal producer of thought-bubbles, there is a perpetual talker in our minds, and it thinks that it has to have something to do — or at least something to talk about. If it hasn't anything else, it natters away making lists and suggesting likely and unlikely plans for the future. Active techniques give it various things to work on — a word, a sound (mantra), a mental image (mandala), or an object upon which to concentrate. In passive exercises, we are trying to keep the perpetual talker still by letting our awareness rest on the thought-bubbles.

Both types of exercises are aimed at producing an inner silence. In a passive exercise, we ask the perpetual talker to be still while we attend to the thought-bubbles, but since we are really not getting involved with these thoughts, the mind eventually stops producing them for a few moments. If the perpetual talker is silent at that time, we have that very rare thing — a true, deep silence in the mind, and we become like a still, deep sea.

On the other hand, in an active exercise we are asking the bubble producer to be still while we give the perpetual talker something to do. It is very happy to have our undivided attention, but since the job we have given it is so very, very boring, it too eventually falls silent for a time. If the bubble producer is quiet at that time, we again have that miraculous silence. Thus, we may cleverly use these two sources of disturbance to cancel each other out — when everything goes well.

In considering which type of technique is best for you, ask yourself which will be easier for you to control — the thought-bubbles or the perpetual talker — then choose the exercise which attends to the other one. If, for example, you find it fairly easy to silence the commentary that seems to go on in our minds (the Yogis call it the 'monkey mind'), but your thoughts frequently skitter off into unexpected directions, you might choose the passive technique.

Another factor to consider is whether you are an active or a passive person. If you are an introverted person and it is easier for you to watch the world go by in a passive way than it is to take an active part in it, the passive technique might be easier for you, whereas an extrovert would probably find the active techniques easier. On the other hand, if you are already using a technique that is in character in this respect, you might want to try the one that is out of character in order to develop more balance in yourself. It is all a question of what you feel most appropriate for you at this time.

Most of the techniques in this book are active — that is, they have a definite focus of attention, rather than just being open and receptive.

Active Exercise

3. Sit. Relax. Count your breaths (each inhale and exhale as one breath) up to ten and then begin at 'one' and count them again up to ten. Repeat again and again through the practice time. When you lose count, start again.

Do not try to control your breathing in any way.

As you can see, 'active' does not mean 'controlling'. It is simply having a focus with which you actively engage your awareness, rather than the reflective waiting of the 'passive' technique.

Passive Exercise

4. Sit. Relax. Tell yourself that you are now going to relax mentally and let your mind drift, not thinking about anything in particular. Allow thoughts to form and to fade again without thinking about them in an analytical way or trying to control them. Let them be like bubbles rising up from the depths, and let them drift away again. You are just observing them come and go.

When the practice time is up, you can review these thoughts, if you wish, and see if any of them suggest insights into your attitudes and or behaviour patterns, but do not think about that while you are practising.

10. Sensation or Mentation?

Yet another way of looking at the variation of techniques is to divide them into sensory and mental categories. Generally speaking, exercises that concentrate our attention on our breath, or other physical processes, help us to be more centered and earthed. They encourage us to be less vague and unfocused, both in our practice and in our daily life, and if this is a problem for you, you may want to choose a sensory focal point.

On the other hand, if you have problems with your breathing or discomfort in your body, it may be helpful to you to move your attention entirely away from it by choosing a mental focus. Surprisingly, this often results in a body that is relaxed and healthier, simply because an over-active or anxious mind is no longer keeping it tense and disturbed.

Mental Exercise

5. Sit. Relax. Choose a colour such as green, blue, lavender, or blue-violet. Think of a sphere of this colour and visualise it during your practice period.

Do not choose an active, energetic colour such as red, yellow, or orange.

Different colours, like different sounds, have varied effects on your system. Use your intuition to choose the right colour for yourself.

The mental exercises are not necessarily complex, although some quite advanced exercises may be. The only difference between them and the sensory exercises is that the mental ones ignore the body, while the sensory techniques use a particular aspect of physical being, often the breath, as a focal point.

Sensory Exercise

6. Sit. Relax. Become aware of your breath. Notice the inhalation, notice the exhalation. Now begin noticing the shift where the breath changes from inhalation to exhalation, from exhalation to inhalation. Be attentive to those shifts. Do not extend them or try to emphasise or control them in any way — just be aware of them. Count these shifts up to ten, then begin your count again. Repeat this throughout the meditation period.

Alternative: *To make this exercise more of a challenge, don't count. Just note the shifts of the breath and keep your mind wholly focused on that.*

The first version is suitable for beginners, the second for those with more experience.

11. Will or Surrender?

Some of the exercises emphasise 'being in control' — disciplining our thoughts and/or our bodies — while others concentrate on simple awareness, on being fully present and attentive in the moment. The 'will' exercises help us to be more disciplined and in control of ourselves, while the 'surrender' exercises help us to be less controlling, just asking us to observe a natural process or to be attentive without controlling anything. Ask yourself if you are over-controlled and rigid? Or perhaps too yielding, even floppy? Is it easy for you to make your own choices, or do you wait until outside forces seem to make them for you?

There is a story about a Yogi who met a Sufi poet one day. The Yogi wanted to prove how well Yoga had worked for him (still a bit of an ego problem there), and he handed the Sufi a sword, telling the poet to strike him hard with it. The poet demurred, but the Yogi insisted. Finally the Sufi struck the Yogi and the sword bounced off him. He struck again several times, at the insistence of the Yogi, and each time the sword rebounded, as if from steel, leaving the Yogi unharmed.

Then the Sufi handed the sword back to the Yogi, asking to be struck with it himself. The Yogi was very much against doing this, knowing that the Sufi had not been trained in Yoga. However, he was finally persuaded. He brought the sword down on top of the poet's head. To his astonishment and dismay, the sword passed cleanly through the Sufi, without meeting any resistance, and came to rest in the ground between the poet's feet. The Sufi smiled and bowed to the Yogi before walking away.

Some of these exercises strengthen us more in one way, some in another. Rather than trying to emphasise one aspect of ourselves to the detriment of another, it may be best to choose the one that is going to help us to develop a better balance in ourselves. Then we can be flexible when adaptability is appropriate and can stand our ground firmly when that is the best response, but we are not locked into one response or one belief system like the Yogi of the story.

Will Exercise

7. *Sit. Relax. Choose a two- or three-syllable sound which has no meaning to you but which is a pleasant sound. Use the same sound each time. Repeat the sound over and over, aloud or silently, or alternately silently and aloud.*

If you are doing it aloud, let the sound rise up from your lower abdomen.

Different sounds affect us in a variety of complex ways. Use your intuition to help you select the sounds that will be most helpful in creating harmony in your system.

In the will exercises, we choose a focal point and stay with it, bringing ourselves back each time we stray. However it should be noted that this is done with gentle firmness, not with anger or force. We are simply exercising our power to choose what we want to be doing or thinking — we are not imposing our will *over* someone or something. In the surrender exercises, we simply observe an existing natural process, attending to it with concentrated awareness.

Surrender Exercise

8. *Sit. Relax. Be aware of your breath. Observe the sensation of inhalation and exhalation. See how continuously and how closely you can observe and sense your own breath. Be aware of the movement of the air through the nostrils, the throat, and in the lungs. Be aware of the movement of your chest and abdomen as you breathe. Keep your undivided attention on your breath.*

Do not attempt to change or control your breath in any way — simply observe it.

12. Doing or Non-Doing?

The non-doing techniques are those that have no focal point other than stillness — and even stillness is not the focus. Simply being focused is the focus. These techniques are usually very difficult for most people and generally are more suitable for someone who has been practising for a while. Not thinking of anything, not even of 'not thinking' is quite a mental balancing act. In describing non-doing there is a Zen saying: *I am not thinking! I am not not-thinking!*

Although one of the aims of meditation is to experience what happens when the mind is in completely concentrated stillness and the body relaxed, most techniques allow it to happen when the mind is ready rather than actively pursuing it. I have included one Non-Doing exercise here and an additional one in Appendix A so that you might try them, but most people will find them very difficult. If you have never tried to meditate before, you may be amazed at just how hard they are.

Remember: your mind is to be still — not thinking about being still, not noticing anything you hear, not noticing your body. It is the direct and immediate experience of nothing, resting in nothingness, like the silent moon resting in space, and the moon then disappears, leaving nothing resting in nothingness. Yet it becomes more than that. When we do experience complete inner silence, we seem to open up to a completely new realm of being. Rather than the experience of nothingness, we seem to experience everything — an everything that is undifferentiated, not separate, not even one thing distinguishable from another. Instead of emptiness, we have infinite fullness.

Mystics throughout the ages have tried to describe this experience in art and poetry and literature, but it is indescribable. Some people regard this experience as a mark of divine favour, and at the other extreme, some regard it as an aberration of the brain. It has been interpreted in all sorts of ways over the ages, in the light of various religions and theories, but as an experience it just *is*. We cannot usually make it happen — in fact, trying to make it happen can be one way of blocking it (although some

Zazen techniques use the frustration of *trying* to create a state in which the mind finally does break through into the silence, becoming open and still).

We are back to the idea we found in the word *contemplate* — the creation of an open space in the mind. In this open space, we may experience the ineffable. One who practises usually has this experience sooner or later (sometimes much later), but making it a goal of your meditation is a mistake. For now, what you need to know is that these open spaces in the mind can happen in the practice of any technique, and that they can (and often do) happen outside of meditation, but they usually happen sooner and more often to people who meditate.

Doing Exercise

9. Sit. Relax. Imagine a circular pool of water in your mind. See it with your mind's eye. Imagine the pool being utterly still, without a ripple to disturb the surface. Hold your attention on keeping the surface still, imagining that any thoughts or distractions cause ripples or waves. When you find yourself thinking of anything else, smooth out the surface of the water again.

Nearly all meditation techniques are 'doing'. The instructions for a pure 'non-doing' exercise would be something like: Sit. Allow yourself to be without thought, without feeling, without sensation, without sensory impressions. The exercise below gives you a running start by beginning as 'doing' and gradually moving into 'non-doing'.

Non-Doing Exercise

10. Sit. Relax. Visualise one of the quiet colours such as blue. Picture the blue shrinking down to a dot and then disappearing altogether, leaving your mind a blank. Stay completely blank. When you find yourself thinking of something, start again with the colour, and let it disappear into nothing.

This exercise is usually not recommended for beginners.

13. Final Choice

Choosing the best path for yourself may seem complicated at the moment, but it is about to become more simple. First, try any of the techniques given above that appeal to you for about ten minutes each. There are additional meditation techniques, from which you may choose, given in Appendix A. There is also a table in Appendix B, showing all the techniques, listed by the categories discussed above, for easy reference. If you wish to use this table, simply make a list of the categories you want and see which technique comes closest.

After you have tried a variety of exercises and have a better sense of what works for you, select the one with which you think you would like to work. When you have made your choice, stick with it for at least three months, even if it seems (as it most likely will at times) difficult or if it seems non-productive. Try to avoid changing and changing again to find an easier way — there probably isn't one. The problems we have are very rarely with the actual exercises themselves; nearly always the problem is resistance within us.

Some of these exercises are obviously more difficult than others; some are recommended for complete novices, some for those who are more experienced. Try to choose one that gently challenges you, but that isn't so difficult that you become discouraged enough to give up practising. You do not get any extra points for trying to do something that is too hard for you! *This is not a contest* — but inevitably it is a check on your self-awareness, and it's an opportunity to exercise your sense of what is right for you at this time.

If, after reading all this, you are still confused about which technique would be best for you, toss a coin to decide. It matters less *which* exercise you do than that you do one — and do it consistently. Any of them will help you and will be far, far better than none. There is no *wrong* technique — only good, even better, and best-for-the-moment. None of them will ever be a waste of your time.

14. Staying on the Path

Keeping on track is one of the most difficult aspects of our inner journeys. We keep finding tempting byways, or we stop and become involved in some interesting local activity we have found. During the practice of any technique, it is very important to keep our minds awake and attentive and in focus. The *body* is supposed to be deeply relaxed, the *mind* alert and aware, but not tense. There should be a kind of attentive tautness, a wide-awake, focused awareness. If you find that you have semi-dozed through your practice, you need to find ways to stay more alert. I am not suggesting that you do anything quite so radical as the custom in many Zen monasteries of having a monitor to whack you on the shoulder with a wooden stick to help you maintain alertness, but you do need to keep a clear, bright focal point.

If the meditation is about listening, listen with your whole self. If it is about seeing, see with your whole self, body, mind, and emotions. Let every part of you attend to the focal point of the meditation. Allow yourself to become one with what is seen or heard or held in the mind or with the breath so that all else drops away. This is not a 'try to' thing, but just something that you gently do, bringing yourself more and more into one concentrated point of focus.

The point of the exercises is to bring your mind into a single focus — and this does not happen if you are dozy and only half there. People sometimes get the idea that 'relaxed' necessarily means 'half asleep'. Think of a cat relaxed on a window ledge, watching the world. It is relaxed, but fully alert — as we realise when a dog appears and we see the cat's lightning response. In our practice we expect to experience physical relaxation combined with mental alertness so that, like the cat, we have an instant awareness of the intruders in our mind.

When you need to sleep, sleep. When you want to meditate, meditate!

When you find that your mind has wandered off somewhere (and it inevitably will, often), gently bring yourself back to the exercise. 'Gently' is the important word — don't slide off into frustration or anger at yourself. These are non-productive emotions and just another form of distraction. Simply bring yourself back, and continue. Be aware, as you do this, that each distracted part of you comes back and joins in the meditation, until all of you is involved. Be like the string of a well-tuned instrument, still, taut but not tense, attuned, waiting in silence for the note to be sounded.

There are a several skills and techniques that may help you with your meditation practice. Let's take a look at some of them.

Part III

On Useful Things to Know

15. Scheduling Our Journeys

Timing is an important factor in any journey. When we leave, how long we travel, and when we plan to return are all important considerations. Each journey affects the subsequent ones as we build up strength, stamina, and experience.

A person who can meditate for as long as thirty seconds without interruption when he first begins is both unusual and fortunate. Most people are astonished to find how short a time they can actually focus their attention without distraction. For the beginner, a meditation period of five minutes, twice a day, is probably long enough for the first week. You don't wish to condition yourself to find meditation a frustrating experience, and it is easy to do just that if you attempt to do more than you are ready to do.

After about a week of practising for five minutes twice a day, the time can be increased to ten minutes. This may later be increased to fifteen or even twenty minutes for each meditation period if desirable. For many people ten minutes is ample time, but each of us must determine what suits us best and find out how long it takes for us to receive maximum benefit from the exercise. We may feel we even need to compromise between that and the time we have available to us.

It is also important to see that the length of time spent practising is consistent every day — not five minutes one day, twenty the next, and ten the day after. If you should occasionally wish to meditate longer than usual for some specific reason, it is best to practise for your usual length of time, take a break, and then later do the extra time. Letting ourselves splodge around with our meditation time can encourage a tendency to be 'spacey' or 'drifty', and it leads to having less control over the activities of the mind rather than increasing control. Being able to control *what* our minds are doing is only half of the goal — it is equally important to be able to control *when* they do it.

As we practise our techniques over a period of months and years, there are times when we feel like spending much more time on our meditation. This usually seems to happen when we are undergoing some kind of internal transformation process, and have finally passed through the various layers of resistance. At this point, we may have such a sense of fulfilment and joy from our practice that we wish to spend extra time. There is just one caution here: if you find you wish to spend long hours every day meditating, ask yourself very seriously if you may not be using it as an escape from life rather than as an aid to living in the world more fully and constructively. If the answer is clearly 'no', then the longer meditations you feel like doing are probably entirely appropriate at this time. The test is, is your daily business being adequately attended to?

You may also notice that, after you have been meditating for several months or years, your meditation time naturally seems to extend. Where ten minutes once felt right, twenty minutes or a half an hour — or even longer may seem appropriate. What really matters is quality, not sheer quantity. Ten minutes of fully concentrated focus of mind in a relaxed body is of more value than an hour spent with a wandering mind.

There is one more thing that many people find helpful, and that is to have a regular time for practice each day. This encourages the habit of meditation — and since we are such creatures of habit, we might as well set this trait to work for us sometimes.

16. Establishing a Base

When we set out on any adventure, it helps to feel as secure as possible when we begin. Many people prefer to meditate in the same place each day, feeling that the familiarity and routine helps them. Most people also seem to feel that the place in which they meditate becomes imbued with an 'energy' — a feeling of warmth and stillness and peace that is conducive to meditation. I used to have a favourite chair for meditation, and guests always seemed drawn to that particular chair. Whoever sat in it after dinner usually fell peacefully asleep, often to their own surprise and embarrassment when they awoke. It became known among my friends as 'the Sleeping Beauty Chair'.

For a while I was concurrently involved in running an antique business and teaching meditation. I used one of the rooms in the shop for my classes, and we soon discovered, to our surprise, that we couldn't seem to keep furniture in there, especially chairs. People kept falling in love with them and buying them. Then we would move more chairs into that room, have another class, and people would say things like 'isn't this comfortable' while bouncing gently in a decrepit old thing with broken springs. I never did quite work out the ethics of this.

The thing about all this is that, yes, meditating in a regular place has its value. However, as in all else, it is important that we do not do something that will hinder our being able to meditate whenever and wherever we might need to. By all means, have a regular place if that suits you, but also make sure that you frequently meditate in other places so you don't feel that you can only practise in one spot.

17. Beginning a Journey

Long ago, ships setting out from some Mediterranean ports ritually gave an offering of flowers to the spirits in the sea. We still set out to do things and go places with some kind of comforting ritual. We may go through a mental checklist, go back and double check that we have locked the door, check our wallets or handbags, or say goodbye to the cat. A ritual is a set of actions performed in a particular sequence. The actions themselves may have a practical purpose or not — what makes them into a ritual is that they are done in a set form, and this comforts us and helps us feel in control as we begin something. We tend to feel quite uncomfortable if any of our rituals are scrambled or incomplete.

It is very useful to develop our own ritual or ceremony, a set of signals

that tells our bodies and our minds that it is time to shift into or out of
the meditative state of consciousness. This is like warming up the car or
stretching out before jogging, a way of preparing ourselves for action —
or non-action, as the case may be. Once more, we can use our tendency
to form habits to help us by creating a very brief routine that can be used
as a trigger, a way of shifting into meditation.

In creating our ritual, common sense is important. Obviously,
something long and elaborate is going to be counter-productive. People
who think that they must sit facing the east, must have this brand of
incense burning, must have that white candle in a special holder in front
of them, must sit on a special mat with their crystals arranged in a
particular pattern around them — these people are engaged a kind of
primitive magic. They are trying to bribe or coerce the universe into
giving them something — in this case a blissful meditation — which they
feel they have now paid for. Their energies would be better spent on
diligently attending to their meditation technique.

This sort of thing also gives our resistance a lot of tools with which to
work. If we feel we must do something elaborate in order to meditate,
then we can't meditate when circumstances prevent us from fulfilling our
ritual, can we? We can see then that it is also unwise to include in our
ceremony anything that requires particular objects or circumstances in the
environment, such as the lighting of a candle, or requires that we do
something that we cannot do just anywhere. In creating your ceremony,
ask yourself if you would be able and willing to do this while stopped in
a traffic jam, while sitting in the waiting room of a hospital, while sitting
in a busy airport, or while sitting in the same room as your mother? If
the answer is 'no' to any of these, think of a better ritual.

The ritual can be as simple as a few words and a couple of deep breaths.
The words could be a prayer or can simply state what we want to do, but
it is important to use the same words each time. These words then
become associated with allowing ourselves to drop into that relaxed,
focused state of meditation, and once that association has become firm,
they become a key which opens the door to that state.

When I first began meditating I used a three-fold breath ritual of my
own. On the first breath as I inhaled I thought, 'I am breathing in peace'.
On the exhalation I made an image in my mind of my centre of being

connected to the centre of the earth. On the second breath I thought, 'I am breathing in peace' on the inhalation, and on the exhalation I made an image in my mind of my centre connected to the centre of the universe. On the third breath, I thought, 'I am filled with peace' on the inhalation, and on the exhalation focused my attention in my own centre, feeling its connectedness to earth and heaven, and letting go of everything else. Then I began practising my meditative technique. Over the years this seems to have simplified itself so that it all happens in one slow, deep breath, but this took a long time.

In working out your own ritual, keep it internal, keep it easy to remember — it doesn't help to be sitting there frantically trying to remember what comes next — and keep it gentle. Remember that meditation is not an attack on some part of yourself, but a loving gift you give to yourself.

Keep it fairly short — long-winded rituals get pretty boring after a while, and because they are habit they are hard to give up. Something brief and to the point which involves both the mind and the body is probably the most effective thing.

If you feel a need for protection from anything in your environment, physical or psychic, you might want to visualise yourself surrounded by a pure white light, which shelters and holds you. It also would be a really good idea to practise some of the earthing and centering exercises we will discuss in later chapters.

A ritual for returning to the usual wakened state of consciousness is also valuable. I used concentrating on the inhalation of three deep breaths — the first to say 'thank you' to the powers-that-be and myself, the second to become aware of my body, and the third to become aware of my external environment. Again, in time it has come down to just one breath and the 'thank you' combined with awareness. Then I spend a couple of moments just enjoying being in the world while still fully experiencing all the peace of meditation.

Now, this is not what I believe *you* should say or do — it is just an example which may suggest the general kind of thing you might find useful. It really doesn't matter whether we develop our own rituals, use rituals learned from someone else, or use an adapted version of a learned ritual. It *does* matter that the ritual feels both appropriate and

comfortable and that it is incorporated as an integral part of the
meditative exercise.

18. Staying Awake on the Road

Falling asleep on an inner journey is not dangerous, as it is when driving
a car, but it does mean that we don't go anywhere. One of the problems
often encountered in our practice is that, perhaps tired after a day's work,
we may find we have a tendency to fall asleep shortly after we become
comfortable and shut our eyes. This is hardly surprising — most of us
have spent years trying to condition ourselves to do just that. Also,
certain physical conditions (low blood pressure, anaemia, and low blood
sugar, for example) can exaggerate a tendency to fall asleep when we shut
our eyes. However, there is a simple technique that can be used for
training ourselves to stay awake.

First, position yourself comfortably. You will need to be in an
armchair for this because you'll need a place to rest your elbow at a
comfortable height and angle. When comfortable, you should place your
elbow (either one) on a firm surface and raise your forearm vertically in
the air. In this position your raised forearm and hand can be balanced
easily as long as you remain awake, but will fall if you begin to sleep.

Usually this is enough to waken you. If it fails to do so, the next time
you can try tilting your arm slightly so that it will fall on your body at
or near the solar plexus. This will waken almost anyone — in fact, it is
a pretty jolting experience. If you are tired enough to sleep through being
hit in the solar plexus, you are much too tired to try to meditate. A few
repetitions of this will usually condition anyone to stay awake during
meditation. In fact, if you use this technique to learn to stay awake while
meditating lying down, it will probably condition you to be unable to
sleep at all in that position, so a favourite sleeping position should not be
used.

19. Solitary Travelling

There are both advantages and disadvantages in going it alone as we experiment and find the techniques that work best for us, adapting the techniques of others and inventing new ones for ourselves, if necessary. In doing this, we learn a great deal, both about ourselves and about what we are doing and where we are going with it.

In this book you have not been told that any one particular technique or exercise is the only right way to do something. Rather, you have been asked to try a variety of things and to decide for yourself what is best for you at this time. A choice of exercises has been given, which are all aimed at achieving the inner silence, so that you can choose the one which works best for you. There are several good reasons for making your own choice of meditative techniques rather than having it made for you. There are also good reasons for finding and working with a teacher.

The Advantages

First, and perhaps most importantly, we are individuals and have individual needs. A teacher can advise us, but in the end it is we who make the choice to do the exercises, and it is as well to recognise this from the start. It is important that we take responsibility for ourselves. I have known too many 'students' of meditation who rush from teacher to teacher, technique to technique, waiting for someone to wave a magic wand over them and transform them into enlightened beings. This is not how it works.

No teacher, no technique, no group can make our meditation 'good'. The process happens inside of us and only we can do it. Others may try to suggest helpful things or, alternatively, to discourage us, but the actual experience of meditation cannot be induced from the outside. External influences can, as we will see, affect our meditation, but they can never substitute for sincere and dedicated practice — and that is something we must do for ourselves.

The practice of meditation is a long, hard slog. Even though there are many rewards along the way, there are periods where nothing much seems to happen. There are even periods when our meditation seems to actually become much more difficult, for no visible reason at all. During these times others may encourage us, but it is still we who must persist in our practice. Accepting this responsibility for ourselves and meeting its challenges can be a very powerful aid in developing self-esteem, a sense of self-worth, and self-discipline.

Possibly the most important thing we may learn from supervising our own meditation practice is that there is something in us, an inner teacher, which knows a lot more that we think we know. It lives somewhere on that mountain at the centre of the Sea of Changes, and we can learn to listen to it as it calls directions to us.

The Disadvantages

Of course, the main disadvantage to supervising your own practice is that your teacher doesn't know any more about meditation than you do (although your inner teacher may well know more than you *think* you do). The other primary disadvantage is that there is no one to notice and correct you when you have fallen into poor habits — droopy or rigid posture, lax awareness, sloppy focus. Working with a teacher or a group encourages us to be more aware of what we are doing and provides us with objective feedback from others. There is also the undeniable psychological advantage of having to report on what we have been doing to others. This tends to motivate many of us to practise daily — although it does not, of course, assure that we will. Working with a group on a regular basis means that we actually do meditate when the group meets, however slipshod we may be about it the rest of the time.

In meditation, there always seems to be more to learn, always further to stretch ourselves. A good teacher can usually judge our readiness and unreadiness for new techniques more accurately than we can ourselves.

20. Finding a Guide

In strange territory, a knowledgeable guide is wonderfully reassuring and helpful — if we can find one. There is an old saying that 'when the student is ready, the teacher appears'. This may well be true, but our ideas about readiness and the universe's ideas may differ. And, of course, a part of becoming 'ready' may be the process of searching for a teacher.

The personal qualities of a teacher are important as well as their knowledge of meditation. If their meditation is really working for them, you can tell by their personality. This does not mean that they will necessarily be radiant beings of light (very few are), but that you will probably sense a particular kind of compassion in them. You will also probably feel that they are powerful without feeling they are trying to control or manipulate you.

A good teacher will suggest things for you to try, but will not get angry if you don't do them and will definitely not try to run your life. However, a good teacher may also decide that, if you don't try the things they offer, there is not much point in the two of you continuing to waste time together.

A good teacher may charge you a reasonable (an elastic word, that) amount for their teaching time. Meditation is priceless, but as we know today, time is worth money and people need to earn a living. Something that you are unwilling to pay for is probably not worth much to you. However, having said all that, I would caution you to beware of anyone charging vast sums and offering fast 'enlightenment'. In fact, I wouldn't even bother to go see anyone like that. I would also be very wary of anyone who wanted me to sign a long-term contract for courses or pay very large sums in advance.

Many people who teach meditation techniques do so as a part of a religious philosophy. If it is not your religion, it may all seem a bit weird and, perhaps, even uncomfortable. I would never join a religion just to learn meditation. Other ways are available. If you already are a member of a formal religious group, you might be most comfortable with a teacher of your own religion — whether they teach meditation as a part of a religious practice or not. It is not unreasonable to ask a teacher of meditation what their religious beliefs are and how much religious teachings are involved in their meditation teaching. They may decline to answer the first question, but definitely should answer the second.

If you meditate on your own for a while, you will begin to have a clearer understanding of your own needs and purposes. This clarity could help you in determining whether a particular teacher or a particular type of meditation is appropriate for you. The teacher who is right for you will have a resonance with your own inner teacher, and they will be in harmony with each other, even when you are baffled or frustrated by both of them.

Sometimes we may live in places where such teaching is simply not available. This is true not only for people who live in lighthouses, but also for people who live in communities where no teacher happens to be available. We can still gain some of the benefits of working with others by participating in or forming a meditation group.

21. Sharing the Journey

One of the enjoyable things about travelling is meeting other people who are on the same path. Apart from the simple, but valuable, human companionship involved, we can also learn more about the road, compare paths we have taken and places we have been, and be encouraged and helped by their experiences. Practising meditation with a group on a regular basis is valuable to many people.

There is a kind of resonance that builds up in a group which definitely helps to keep our concentration focused. There is value in being able to discuss your meditation experience with others, learning from each other. Many people also find it much easier to make time for their private practice when they have the psychological support of belonging to a meditation group. Although meditation is essentially a solitary practice, even when done in a group, we are social creatures and often benefit from feeling that we are not going out on a strange limb by ourselves. A group at least helps us to feel that there are others out on the limb with us.

Such a group needs to be chosen carefully. One person suffering from ego problems that make him or her want to run things and tell others what to do can make everyone uncomfortable. One way of avoiding this is to hand the leadership of the group to a different member in a predetermined order each time. Someone does need to be the nominal focaliser for the group. Otherwise, it tends to become just another social evening.

Many groups find that they want to work with a book on meditation, such as this one, reading and discussing a different section each evening so they are certain they all have an understanding of it. They may do this before or after the evening's meditation practice. Other groups like to spend part of their time studying a more philosophical or theoretical book and part of their time meditating together in silence. Some groups just like to meditate in silence and leave in silence. There are all sorts of possibilities, and you are limited only by the desires of your group and the materials available to you.

You also need to decide in advance what your policy is on new members for the group. If you are just meditating, new members can usually fit in quite nicely. If you are studying a particular subject as well as meditating, it may be more difficult. In thinking about this there are two important factors to consider.

One factor is how difficult it would be for an outsider to review and catch up on the work you have done so that they are not constantly requiring that the group go over things that have already been completed. The other factor is that a new member changes the 'energy' of the group. This may be an asset, giving new impetus to a group that has become stodgy or dull, or it may be a problem in some way. This needs group discussion.

When working with a group which discusses meditation as well as meditating together, it seems to be doubly tempting to fall into the trap of having 'wonderful' experiences. This should be most diligently avoided.

22. The Changing Scene

As we travel through any new place, we find unexpected things. Some of these we may enjoy, others we may not. The important thing in this kind of journey is to keep going. Many people, when they first start meditating, have interesting experiences. None of these experiences are 'good' or 'bad'; they are just a part of our personal processes. If we do not understand them we may either become attached to them, because we believe they are something wonderful, or feel concern, because they are unfamiliar. It is always comforting to know what may happen and what, if anything, needs to be done about it.

It is quite likely that you may never have any of these experiences as they usually tend to occur to people who are engaged in an intense meditation programme involving several hours of meditation daily. However, if you do ever experience any of them in a mild form, it's useful to understand what is going on.

Feeling Good

In the early days of meditation people often feel euphoric or uplifted by their practice. There are a lot of possible explanations for this, but one of my favourites is that our minds and bodies are so relieved that we are finally doing this lovely thing for ourselves that they become quite euphoric. After a while they become habituated to that level of relaxation and balance, and then we no longer experience it as especially blissful. We must then reach new depths of relaxation and increased intensity of concentration in order to experience the same depth of sensation.

It is important, however, to remember that the good feelings are not the reason why we meditate. Even the ultimate in good feelings, the mystical experience, is not a goal in itself. It is merely something that fuels us for the next stage of our journey. If we meditate only for bliss, we are likely to be terribly disappointed most of the time.

We must always bear in mind that meditation also promotes relaxation of the body and mind, development of mental concentration and control, reduced stress, balancing of our subtle energies, emotional and mental clarity, enhancement of our self-healing ability, and so on and on. All of these are achieved with or without the feeling of upliftment. That feeling is just a bonus which sometimes occurs to tell us that we are definitely doing A Good Thing for ourselves.

Visions

Another phenomenon many people experience is seeing lovely visions or beautifully coloured lights or hearing exquisite music when they first meditate. People who have this happen may equate 'good' meditation with these phenomena and be disappointed if they fail to have them. People also tend to get into competition about their visionary experiences, which starts them generating fantasies instead of meditation. This competition might be with others, or it might be a more subtle competition with ourselves, trying to top the last 'wonderful' experience.

If you are listening to the music or watching the films in your head, you are probably not attending to your focus, and if you are not attending to your focus, you are not meditating.

If, however, you ignore the phenomena and continue with your meditation, these things will gradually fade away. They seem to mark particular kinds of change in our internal energy balance and also the transitions from one level of consciousness to another, often a deeper level.

Most people who have practised for years have had various phenomena come and go. In some Christian traditions, in Yoga, in Zen Buddhism, and in many other spiritual traditions, these phenomena are considered 'illusions' or 'temptations' — distractions and manifestations of resistance to actual meditation. Some traditions, Tantra Yoga, for example, suggest that you observe the phenomena closely, but do not become attached to or involved with them. An experienced teacher can tell a great deal about how your meditation is going by the kinds of phenomena you do or don't experience.

Lovely as such phenomena may often be, they are only markers along the way, and many people pass those markers *without* experiencing the phenomena at all. The important thing is to regard them as a passing part of a process and to let them go. If we become attached to them and meditate for the purpose of experiencing the phenomena, we go no further. It is like standing and admiring a milepost, thinking that it means we have reached the end of the journey. If we just notice them in passing, let them go, and go on with our practice, they will gradually fade like the transitory phenomena they are. I spent a lot of time in the early months of my practice trying to make sense out of all those lovely colours — time that would have been better spent meditating.

Like the occasional feelings of euphoria, they indicate change and should be valued for that, then released. If we hold onto these phenomena, we cannot go on past them into that deeper level of consciousness and deeper stillness and clarity where these experiences also fall away into silence. These phenomena definitely are not 'goals' for which we should strive.

Emotional Release

People who have been very tense for a long time sometimes find as they relax that various emotions come to the surface. These often are simply the feelings that were locked up, perhaps long ago, in the rigid muscles, and they sometimes bubble up into our consciousness when the tension holding them is released. They are the feelings that were, sometime in the past, wanting to do something that the mind was forbidding. They are old stuff, and they no longer matter — they are just something we need to let go of along with the tension. People who do massage and other types of bodywork are very familiar with this phenomenon.

Sometimes we may feel like crying, we may feel sad or angry. If this sort of thing should ever come up when you are meditating or doing one of the relaxation techniques, don't be deceived by it. Our minds try to explain any feelings we may have by finding a cause for them in the present. For example, a relaxing muscle group may release a feeling of anger, and the mind immediately starts looking for a reason for this anger in the present or the recent past. The Chinese proverb says 'the man who wants to beat a dog can always find a stick' and we can always find someone or something to be angry about — if we look diligently enough. However, the anger itself may not really be about anything in the present; it may only be an 'artifact', something left over from the past with no relevance to our present lives. Such artifacts need to be recognized for what they are and simply released, so that they do not become entangled in our present lives and feelings.

This is certainly not a problem that usually occurs when we relax deeply, but it is something we need to recognise if it does happen. If such emotions do come up, the *Breathing In Truth* exercise (in Part VIII, Chapter 40) can be very helpful. If the exercise restores us to serenity, we know the emotion is just an artifact. If the truth is that we really have something in the present to be emotional about, our feelings will not disappear in the exercise, although attending to our breath will help us to be more calm and objective about it.

Energy Sensations

When meditating or relaxing, we sometimes experience strange sensations of energy moving around in our bodies. These may even be accompanied by muscular twitches or jerks. Such sensations are virtually never actually painful, and they are only of concern to us because they are unfamiliar. These experiences occur, like those of emotional release, because we are letting go of locked-up tensions and freeing the energy in them. In fact, we might call them 'energy release'. They are related to the twitches and jumps we sometimes feel as we go to sleep. It takes energy to maintain tension, and when we release it, it rushes off to find something else to do or to discharge through the system.

We may also experience these sensations outside of our meditation or relaxation time. If you think there might be a real physical problem, check with your doctor, but the energy sensations are probably just old, old tensions letting go and the energy in your body rebalancing. This is another thing that does not happen to a lot of people, but may occasionally occur.

Should these sensations ever be strong enough to bother you, the metaphysician's prescription for reducing them is as follows:

1. Get a good rest every night — go to bed and get up at reasonable and regular hours.

2. Eat sensible food at regular hours — no extreme diets.

3. Get plenty of healthy exercise. This doesn't mean going out and jogging for hours every day if you are accustomed to a sedentary lifestyle — be reasonable and approach any change in your exercise patterns gradually. Things like working in the garden or going for walks in the country are particularly good for this.

4. Don't use drugs, not even prescription ones, unless they are essential to your health. Under these circumstances, drugs will only make you even more weird and confused. Your body is trying to find a healthier balance — give it a chance.

5. Meditate fifteen minutes a day. No more; no less. This helps to stabilise and moderate the rate of change and release.

6. Practise some of the earthing and centering exercises in Parts VI, VII, and VIII every day. The stronger the sensations, the more you need these exercises.

7. Don't get excited about the sensations and don't become attached to the idea that they mean that you are doing something wonderful. They are just mileposts to tell you that you are changing and becoming a more relaxed person.

As you can see, the first four are just common sense. So are the last three, but we don't always think of them that way.

Intuition

After meditating for a time, many people have an increase in the kind of sensitivity that most of us have noticed on occasion. Who hasn't had the experience of hearing the phone ring and thinking (for no logical reason), 'That must be so-and-so' — and been right!

Now, the Spiritualists might say you were learning to hear your guides — though I like to think that any guides of mine would have something better to do than spending their time racing me to the telephone. Some fundamentalist Christians, on the other hand, might say the devil was getting to you. I don't see the connection myself, although I have always thought my telephone bill might be the work of the devil, or at least of a very nasty imp. Some people might even think this discussion belongs in the section on religion, but I don't think so. To me, the whole thing seems much simpler than any explanation which requires the intervention of other (perhaps superior and good, perhaps wicked) beings.

In part, our intuition is the result of the fact that we actually see and hear much more than we *notice*. An example of this unnoticed information is the use of hypnosis to recall the license number of a car involved in an accident by a witness who has no conscious memory of noticing that number. Parts of our minds take in the information ignored by the conscious mind (things like our own body language, the body language of others, and details of the environment, for example).

How many times have you felt uneasy when you were speaking with someone? Perhaps felt that something undefinable was 'wrong'? Often this is a result of another part of your mind being aware that the body language of the other person is giving a message that is different from their words. They might be sounding calm and reasonable and honest, but their body might be subtly saying that they were angry or being untruthful. The part of us that 'speaks' our own body language also 'hears' that of others, but we often are not aware of these subtle signals, other than as a vague feeling. The meditator, because of the quietness in his mind, tends to be more conscious of these subtle sources of information.

On another level, nearly everyone has had experiences, which are inexplicable in ordinary terms, of knowing who is at the door, of thinking of someone you haven't heard from for years and then meeting them 'by coincidence' on the street the same day, of knowing what someone is going to say just before they say it even though they have jumped completely to another subject, of knowing that they will win a raffle before the drawing. We have several words for these phenomena: coincidence, hunch, and intuition are some of the ways we describe them.

Because we don't know *how* it happens (only that it does), we tend to assume that it is some kind of magic or the actions of gods or devils, or as is thought by many in our materialistic age, that it is just illusion (a lie we have told ourselves) or chance. If these things have happened to you, as they have to many, it is hard to believe in the illusion theory, and if they happen often, it becomes increasingly difficult to believe that it is only chance.

When we meditate regularly, our minds gradually begin to clear themselves of some of their chaos and babble. When that happens, we sense these subtle perceptions more clearly and more frequently. This worries some people, but it is a perfectly natural process, and we simply need to learn to handle it in the same way that we learned to sort and understand our visual, auditory and kinesthetic impressions as infants and small children.

Our senses seem to work on two levels: physical and energetic (for lack of a better word). Actually, our sight and hearing are also based on the perception of energy — light waves and sound waves. Just because we have not yet understood *how* our 'energetic' senses work does not mean that there is not a perfectly natural explanation. We are aware of our physical senses from birth, although it does take us a while to learn to use them, and even longer to sort out what the input actually means. Our energetic senses are much more subtle and are subject to interference from our emotions and attitudes.

The same ethics and common sense rules apply to the use of our energetic senses as do to our ordinary senses, and we need to remember that the same gap exists between perception and understanding that exists in the ordinary world. In the ordinary world, a stranger may spend the night at our neighbour's house while her husband is away. If we don't know that he is her brother, we may leap to some pretty silly conclusions. We need to be doubly careful with the conclusions we draw from our energetic sense perceptions, because until we learn how to properly recognise and evaluate them, we cannot accept them as unquestionably valid information.

As well as being a result of clearing our minds and becoming more aware, sensitivity can also be a result of inadequate grounding and of being off-centre. Many 'natural sensitives' are in this condition, which is why they often have a reputation for being such unstable and unreliable people with weird ideas. Such an unbalanced sensitive usually cannot distinguish clearly between the energetic senses and their own or others' fantasies. Until we have learned how to be thoroughly earthed and centered and to really understand these senses, we would do well to take any such perceptions with a grain of salt and not become attached to or excited about them.

All of the experiences we have discussed in this chapter are leading in one direction: improved physical health, increased mental acuity, greater insight, and a healthier and more balanced emotional state. However, they are only *leading toward* something, not telling us we have already arrived.

23. Noticing Changes

When we are on the move, we don't always notice changes in ourselves as they are happening — yet this is one of the most interesting and important things about any journey. We have discussed several changes which we expect to experience in ourselves when we regularly practise meditation. People often want to know how soon they can expect such benefits for themselves.

The actual changes seem to start right away, but none of them are something that either *is* or *is not*. Pregnancy is an example of that kind of yes/no thing. One either is or is not; one is never a little bit or somewhat pregnant. However, all of the things we have discussed — such as decreased stress, increased energy, improved self-awareness, and so on — extend over a continuum, an unbroken line ranging from 'least possible' at one end to 'most possible' at the other.

The length of time required to achieve changes perceptible to the meditator depends on such things as previously learned habits, the physiological and psychological constitution of the individual, the self-discipline, consistency, and enthusiasm with which the individual practises the exercises, and on the degree of self-awareness of the meditator. And these things are all beneficially affected by meditation, so the longer you do it, the more quickly you can expect to notice change in yourself.

Many people find that keeping a journal is helpful. Probably there is no great value in trying to record our feelings about every meditation, but it is often useful to write a bit regularly about what we are currently experiencing in our practice. We might want to include things like whether or not we generally feel quite relaxed at the end of meditation, whether or not we feel that we are more able to keep our attention on our technique, and whether or not we feel that there is any change in our general response to stress. We might want to note phenomena we have encountered. We may also want to mention any other changes we feel that we are noting in ourselves or that people around us have mentioned.

It may also be useful to keep a note in the journal of the things in ourselves that we would like to change. Be as specific about these things as possible. One of the things that happens to humans is that they tend to forget about anything that is no longer a problem. We may be concerned about our habit of irritation with a particular person or situation, but we rarely notice when we stop feeling that way. Keeping a journal helps us to observe these little and sometimes subtle changes in ourselves. It is especially useful if we are meditating on our own, without the guidance of a teacher or the support of a group.

24. The Experienced Traveller

If we have been passing through the same kind of landscape for quite a while, we tend to become less observant and alert. We think we have seen it all before and plod along without real attention. When we have used the same meditation exercise for a long period of time, it may eventually become less useful — simply a way of relaxing — and it no longer 'stretches' and energises us.

This is why, in many meditation traditions, the student is given progressively more difficult exercises over the years of training. If you are acting as your own teacher, you may feel that the time has come to move onto something a little more difficult, something that stretches you a bit further. For example, if you have always used an inner focus technique, you might want to try one of the outer ones. They are usually a bit more challenging.

There is an alternative. We can use the familiarity and boredom to spur us on to new levels of awareness and intensity of concentration. We can rise above our temptation to sink down into the familiar. If we once found the meditation technique we are using richly rewarding, we might look to ourselves and see if we can regain the enthusiasm and attentiveness we once put into it before we try anything else. If the problem is in us, rather than in the technique, we need to change ourselves rather than it.

25. Setting Goals

Inner journeys of this nature are made *for the sake of the journey itself* — not for some imaginary goal at the equally imaginary end. Meditation is part of a life-long process. The only way we can 'fail' with our meditation exercises is to not do them. We can also inhibit the amount of benefit we may obtain from doing them by constantly criticising ourselves for not 'succeeding' at meditation. Self-criticism, impatience, frustration all work against us, they are both self-created and unnecessary. Success is easy — it is just taking time to do our practice every day.

Regular practice is *in itself* success.

Every society has its own attitudes about setting goals. In our culture at the present time, we seem to like quick goals, and we tend to measure 'success' by how fast we reach them, and we become upset and discouraged if they take 'too long' to achieve. It rarely seems to occur to us that the real goal in meditation, as in many other things, may be to *experience the process* rather than to reach some preselected point. Meditation is a life-long process; there is always more to be learned, more to be experienced, more inner growth to nurture.

If we must set meditation goals for ourselves, we must be careful in the beginning to set only the simple ones of feeling better, feeling more relaxed, feeling that we have more energy, and perhaps feeling that we are gaining more insight into ourselves and others. Then we have goals that begin to show 'success' in a very short time. It would be better to think of these things as 'milestones' rather than as goals, because they simply are an indication that we are coming along well.

One of the things I have learned in my years of teaching is that, if students tell themselves that meditation is not 'successful' unless they actually completely still the mind and experience something exciting, they make it very difficult for themselves to feel that they are getting anywhere with their practice. There are a couple of reasons for not setting such high goals for ourselves.

For one thing, we don't know that we are about to still the mind until it actually happens, so we don't recognise its approach until we are suddenly there — and even then we may not immediately recognise it when it does happen. In many cases the first flickers of silence in the mind are devalued by assuming that we must have been asleep for a moment because there was a time when we were neither hearing nor thinking nor dreaming.

On the other hand, we may think we must have been in the silence when we were actually focused deeply in an altered state of consciousness, thinking about or perceiving something else (or perhaps asleep), and we have no memory of it when we come back. There is a difference. If we have been asleep or thinking in an altered state of consciousness, we will usually feel rested. If we have been in the true silence, we will feel very well rested, energised, uplifted, and possibly even inspired.

In this question of appropriate goals, there is also an issue about cultural expectations. St. Teresa of Avila is said to have claimed that anyone with serious intent can achieve this inner silence within six months to a year. This statement has influenced a lot of people, even people who have never heard it in that exact form or known its source. It is probably true, but we get ourselves into trouble with this idea if we do not understand it within the context of her thirteenth-century culture and expectations.

To St. Teresa, 'serious intent' would almost certainly involve joining a monastery and devoting many of our waking hours to the *Opus Dei,* the 'work of God', the divine office of formal prayer. It would also include further hours each day of private contemplative prayer. And, of course, the rest of our time would be devoted to achieving the open-to-God, contemplative state of mind in all of the ordinary activities of the daily life of a contemplative monk or nun. Most of us now might find that a bit extreme, but to St. Teresa, in her time and milieu, it was an obvious assumption.

In St. Teresa's day, people were prepared to work on a single example of their craft for many years. A cathedral might take generations to build, and one man could easily spend his entire working life upon one small part of it. A landowner planted oaks that would be harvested by his many-times great-grandson. Homes were built to be lived in by generation after generation. Most people just do not think that way any longer. To us, a long-term goal is something that we probably expect to have within a few months or years; to St. Teresa and to many generations before and after her, a long-term goal was often a lifetime commitment, sometimes even a project that would not be completed within the expected life'ime of a grandchild.

In modern conditions, comparatively few people are prepared to completely devote their lives to achieving long-term spiritual goals. Today's long-term goals are mostly things like paying the mortgage, paying the children's university fees, planning for retirement. As a society, we have forgotten what it means to plan far ahead, to consider generations yet unborn; we look for the fast pay-off. A terrible witness to this is the way we have been polluting the earth since the Industrial Revolution, resulting in the ecological crisis we now face.

This whole question of short-and long-term goals may be something you would like to consider in your life, but please don't start by setting yourself up to 'fail' with meditation. If we can confine our lust for setting goals for our meditation to the simple ones of gradually feeling more relaxed and clear, we soon see pleasing results. Most of the positive benefits of meditation described earlier, including the process of personal growth, can be and nearly always are obtained long before you achieve that inner silence.

What really matters, though, is that you practise every day. *That is successful meditation.* People who do so eventually experience the total inner silence, and they often find the ecstasy of the mystic in that silence — but that is not the goal either. The magic word is 'process' not 'goal', and processes just go on — and on.

If we meditate *expecting* a sense of upliftment or ecstasy or some other phenomena, we feel that many of our meditations are 'failures', and we usually become discouraged and stop. It is so important to remember that *doing the meditation is what counts*, not what we experience or even how we feel when we have finished.

In all of the traditions of meditation, Christian and others, teachers speak of times when all our efforts seem to produce nothing, to seem to be mere mechanical acts which we repeat again and again. They call this 'spiritual dryness' and it is recognised that persistence in our meditation practice during these times is the best course. We almost inevitably go through periods when we meditate daily without any visible result — although the negative results are quickly evident if we stop! It is really best if we can simply not judge our meditation experience. We are usually neither objective nor knowledgeable enough to make worthwhile evaluations. And there are better things we can do with our energy — things like practising our meditation technique.

The real aim of meditation practice is to be without goals, without pressure, without striving, without thought — to be effortless and free of our mental and emotional fixations about ourselves. We just need to be alertly focused and waiting in serene stillness. The key word here is 'being', not 'doing'.

26. Travelling with an Open Heart

When we travel, what paths we follow, with whom we share the journey, are all, in a way, incidental to the process. What really matters on an excursion of this kind is how open we are to new experience and growth. There is a simple thing we can do to enhance this openness. Many people seem to believe that detachment from all emotion is the ideal in meditation. Most meditative techniques either use something abstract (a word or an image-mandala) or something physical (breath, heartbeat) for the one-pointed focus. The implication (sometimes it's even stated) is that emotion has no place in meditation. This is true, mostly.

Many emotions arouse us — anger, fear, greed, envy, anxiety, excitement, distress, exuberance, bitterness, eagerness, agitation, sorrow, hysteria, delight, smugness, annoyance, misery, chagrin, sympathy, elation, lust, glee, amusement. While these emotions may or may not be pleasurable in themselves, they distract us from the calmness needed to attain the meditative state. On the other hand, feelings such as patience and serenity can be a positive asset. There is a Zen Buddhist meditation technique called *shikan-taza* which uses a specific emotion as a part of its focus.

In this technique, we let our awareness rest in a feeling, the feeling of 'expectant gratitude'. The 'expectant' part is the expectation that we shall fully experience our true nature — open and silent, serene and joyous, filled with light. The 'gratitude', of course, is for experiencing this. Since we *know* that this is our true nature, that we will experience it, and that all we need to do is sit in stillness, there is no hurry or striving or anxiety; there is only serene patience and expectant gratitude, combined with alert awareness.

Choosing to make expectant gratitude a part of our meditation does interesting things. It is amazing and horrifying how easily we slip from expectant gratitude to 'anticipatory pessimism'. We do not even need to be particularly pessimistic as a rule for this to happen. There is something inside many of us, perhaps dormant for the most part, that says it is not-OK to anticipate actual generosity from the universe.

Meditating in expectant gratitude is an exercise in trustingness. Through it we may discover that the *absence* of conscious distrust in our minds is not necessarily the same as the *presence* of real trust. It is interesting that, for so many of us, choosing to experience a strong and deliberate presence of loving trust within ourselves can evoke a response from our unconscious minds of disquiet and vague, unfocused alarm. Most of us have unconsciously accepted the belief that we must go out and struggle for what we want. It is very hard to believe that something wonderful might be there in us. Making the feeling of expectant gratitude a part of our practice gives us a chance to change the habit of suspicion with which we may unconsciously view the universe.

We also seem to believe in a kind of primitive magic that says if I am seen to be desperately anxious and needy and if I try very, very hard and if I hurt a lot, something will be kind to me. We believe we can bribe the universe or others into treating us nicely. This is, of course, just superstition where the universe is concerned and is, at best, unreliable where other people are involved. This belief is a result of our reactions to the experience of life, our projections of our own attitudes onto the universe, but it is not something we need to live with forever if we don't want to. It is just another habit, and as we know, habits can be changed.

One thing we need to realise is that we have the capacity to feel any emotion at any moment. To deny or suppress an emotion that we are feeling can be harmful to us, but at the same time we need not be the slaves of our feelings. We need to look at any present emotion and understand whether it is really based on what is happening right now or if it is just a habit. If it is just a habit, there are dozens of books of techniques and lots of therapists available to help us change it. On the other hand, if the emotion is based on the present situation, we still have the option of changing our response to that situation. In making this change, we may need help.

We don't want to suppress our emotions. When we do that, they form a toxic waste, mouldering in our psyches and creating rotten places. However, we can often learn to respond to things in a new way that does not involve repression, but does involve understanding ourselves and others better. The realignment of our emotions comes naturally with that understanding. This may take a lot of effort, and we may want professional help as we do it, but it is entirely possible.

Since the capacity to feel any emotion is there, latent within us, we can often choose, when we are not completely wrapped up in another feeling, to experience a particular emotion simply by putting our attention on that part of our psyche, as it were. If we think fearful thoughts, we begin to *feel* frightened; if we think angry thoughts, we begin to feel angry; if we think about pleasurable things, we begin to feel pleased or happy. Far more than we realise, our feelings are a matter of choice, and the choice is in what we choose to think about. Habits are choices made while sleepwalking.

We need to understand that when we prepare to meditate, centering, earthing and calming ourselves, we can go one step farther and *choose* to feel expectant gratitude while we practise. This can be a part of almost any meditation technique.

This seems an obvious choice, yet it is one we often do not make. We have something in us called 'resistance', and the next thing we need to do is to have a good look at it.

Part IV

On Going Astray

27. Losing the Way

It's extremely easy to go off course as we meditate. There are several reasons for this, and one of the most common is resistance. Resistance is a special kind of thing we do that involves splitting ourselves in two — a mugger and a victim. The mugger is our unconscious resistance and the victim is the intention or purpose, with which we identify.

For example, when I was fourteen months old, I didn't like porridge, but my mother believed it was good for me. One morning, when she went into the kitchen to get the porridge, I climbed down out of my high chair. She came back to find me standing there and asked me to get back up in the chair.

"Can't," I said.

"Why not?" she asked.

"Can't pick up my foot."

"Why can't you?"

"'Cause my other foot is standing on it."

Resistance is about standing on yourself and then saying you can't move. It also seems to be about acting as if there were really nothing one could do about the situation — as if one were confronted with an immovable obstacle, quite beyond human control. We won't get far on our journey that way.

If these exercises are so easy and if they are so good for us, why, one may ask, doesn't everyone do them?

The reason we don't is because they actually do work. They bring us into close contact with that hardest person of all to face — ourselves — and they change us.

But isn't that the point of it all?

Yes, but these changes are not only the observable things we have already mentioned. They also lead to deeper changes — changes in the way we *unconsciously* think about ourselves and others and in the way we pursue our goals. Sometimes there may even be changes in our fundamental *unconscious* beliefs about the nature of reality. These things are much more than mere changes — they are transformations.

Once we have decided to meditate, many people are surprised at how difficult it actually is to put that intention into practice. Although we are accustomed to 'changing our minds' fairly freely, we rarely change our underlying beliefs about ourselves and about the nature of reality. We often have a lot of 'ego investment' in these beliefs, and they are the things that we accept without question, the things which we always *assume* to be true.

When we change these, we shift the foundations of our world. When that happens, our whole lives take on a different meaning — we may have different desires and we are virtually different people. These unconscious beliefs are also tied up in our assumptions about what we need to do to survive in this world. It is no wonder that we have resistance to this process.

One of the interesting things about resistance is that it only has power over us as long as we are unconscious of the fact that we are resisting and believe that we have a reasonable explanation for our behaviour. We have to be unconscious of our real motivation in order for resistance to work. Once we see that we are not doing what we want to do because a little part of us is frightened, we are apt to go ahead and do it anyway. So resistance, being fairly clever after all, comes disguised in various ways.

We have a wonderful variety of resistance techniques at hand. Resistance usually comes in layers — if one tactic doesn't work, the unconscious may try another. The first step in resistance to meditation usually happens before we even sit down. We hear ourselves making such excuses as:

I just don't have time. Come now! Not have ten minutes for yourself sometime during the course of the day? If you truly don't have ten minutes during the day for yourself, there is probably something wrong with your schedule, but even more, something is wrong with your attitude toward yourself.

I probably can't do it anyway, which is closely allied to *It probably wouldn't do me any good anyway*. Sure. Pretty feeble. I remember hearing someone in a class apologise to their partner for not being able to do the exercise they were supposed to be working on. When I went over to see what the problem was, I found that she hadn't yet tried to do it and didn't intend to because she 'knew' she couldn't. I suggested that she first try it and wait until she had actually failed before she gave up and apologised. Of course, she did the exercise quite well and wound up feeling very pleased with herself.

The children might need me. Of course they might. Or the phone might ring or the house might catch fire or the world might end. Or they might not need you, or at least not need you enough to justify interrupting you. Unless you have an unconscious programme that requires that the children need you all the time, thus proving that you are important enough to be allowed to continue to exist, this idea that you cannot find ten minutes for yourself during the day is obviously not very valid — and in any case, it is not very realistic.

It is also possible to practise while the children are asleep. Some people meditate as a family, including even the smallest children, who very quickly learn what is expected of them.

I'm too tired to meditate properly by the time I finish everything else. Meditation could be allowed a higher priority than that. Many people actually get up a little early so they can practise before they do 'everything else'. They do this because they know that the 'everything else' will go more smoothly and efficiently after they have meditated.

It's never quiet enough around here to meditate. This is probably untrue, but in any case, we will deal with this one later.

In the early days of meditation, we may come back to these Level One resistances again and again. In fact, we may even hear some of the following from people who have been practising for a long time.

I can't keep my mind still — I just can't meditate at all. Well, of course, we can't keep our minds still. If we could, we wouldn't need to meditate.

The whole point of doing the exercises is in training ourselves to *become* still and focused. If we could really do that, with no 'monkey mind' stuff going on in our heads, we would be *living in a meditative state* and we wouldn't need to practise the exercises — except perhaps to keep ourselves reminded of what we are supposed to be doing.

I've been meditating for three days now, and it hasn't done me the least bit of good. The key word here is 'patience'. Very few exercises or practices make much noticeable difference in a few days — or even weeks. People also may say, *I've been meditating for three years now, and it hasn't done me the least bit of good.* This is almost certainly a flat untruth. No one meditates for three years unless they are getting something of value from it. This is nearly always just an excuse to justify stopping, and our real reason for stopping at that moment is probably that we are coming too close to transformation.

The other thing about this is that it is difficult to notice a *gradual* change in ourselves. We may not notice that, over a period of weeks or months, we have begun to sleep better, to feel calmer, to have more energy, to see things more clearly, to be less stressed. Other people often notice the change in us before we do.

I don't know what to expect. I don't think I'm getting anything out of it (or I'm not doing it right). Sometimes people expect bells to ring, choirs of angels to sing, beautiful visions, brilliant insights and ideas, complete bliss, and flashing neon lights spelling out the words 'thou art an illumined being'. If any of those things are happening, *do not stop practising the exercises.* Just observe the experience while you keep your your attention on counting your breath or doing whatever your exercise is. Visionary experiences are all very well and they may or may not mean anything important, but they are a by-product of meditation, and not its purpose. In fact, they are often nothing more than another form of distraction.

Often, we may find that, if we have a problem and we put it aside while we practise our technique, sometime later in the day we are quite likely to have a sudden insight or realisation that clarifies the situation for us — but we are not meditating for that purpose.

When we are meditating, it is helpful to expect nothing and just simply do the exercise. If we are doing the exercise, we are doing the right thing.

*I'm just too lazy (*or *don't have the self-discipline) to do it.* Self-discipline isn't something we have or don't have; it's something we *develop* in ourselves. Like a muscle, it is something that becomes stronger when we exercise it. A lack of self-discipline is not an excuse; it is a statement of a temporary and correctable condition. What we are saying is that we have one foot on top of the other again.

Nearly all Level One resistance ideas are as obviously fallacious as the ones above — from an objective point of view. This kind of resistance only works as long as we think we are being logical and reasonable. As soon as we admit that it is simply resistance, it falls apart — and may then move to Level Two resistance.

For most of, us the next line of defence is physical. The chair is not comfortable, the room is too warm (or too cold), the position we are sitting in uncomfortable, a toe itches, the head aches, a leg has gone to sleep. Again, we just need to recognise that this is simply a form of resistance. Then we can acknowledge it for what it is, deal with any real discomfort, and go on with our meditation. The resistance may stop here, or it may go on to Level Three resistance.

At Level Three it is: Did I remember to turn off the flame under the soup? Did I leave the door open? Did I take the phone off the hook? I forgot to take the coat to the cleaners, I must stop and make a note to remind myself. I forgot to tell my secretary to cancel my appointment with (make an appointment with, send a letter to) Mr. Xyz, I must make a note of that. I'd better pay the electric bill right now, before I forget again. Did I remember to lock the car? I must remember to call my mother (father, doctor, vet, friend, old aunt, plumber). What's that noise outside? Why are the children quiet? Where is the cat? It sounds like those birds are getting into the strawberries again. Did I leave the water on in the bath?

Level Three can also generate lovely little daydreams appearing out of nowhere, and we happily follow these will o' the wisps off our path. These ideas arise like bubbles from the unconscious into the conscious mind, distracting and diverting us. Again, recognition of resistance is required, and we need to continue with our meditation until the planned time is up. Resistance usually gives up at this point or just continues with the same tactics. When we start hitting Level Four resistance, we know we are getting closer to some kind of real change in ourselves.

Level Four is where the resistance gets clever and starts firing Good Ideas into the conscious mind. It's making a real effort now, and we suddenly realise exactly what we need to do about a thing that has been bothering or puzzling us. Unless we are really paying attention at this point, we may well find that we have jumped up and are on our way to do something about it. And the resistance has won. If we really are conscious of what is going on, we simply go on with our meditation — or move to Level Five.

Only on rare occasions is the unconscious mind so upset about our potential change that it goes on to fifth level resistance. Level Five is where the unconscious resistance makes its big effort and gets down to really fighting dirty. Anything, it says, is better than this terrible, threatening meditation stuff and the light it brings into the dark crevices of our minds — so it brings its power to evoke emotion into play. Suddenly, we have this horrible sinking feeling accompanied by some thought, such as: She (he) really doesn't love me. He (she) is probably having an affair with someone else. The boss hasn't said anything, but I know he's unhappy and about to give me the push. I just know I'm going to fail that exam. What if I don't get that contract? What if my son has an accident? What if my wife finds out? What if . . . if . . . if?

This one is harder because our emotions are aroused, but the principle is the same:

Recognise Resistance

This is difficult to do because we *feel* that there is a real problem — it *feels* like something we *know* to be true. This tactic works successfully because it is based on our own insecurities and fears. Our resistance is attacking us where we are most vulnerable. Now, our fears may be based on some kind of objective reality or they may not, but we need to remember is that *what we are hearing is our resistance* — whether it contains any truth or not. The resistance is trying to stop us from practising, and it is desperately hitting below the belt because we are really very close to some sort of a breakthrough. This is the point at which we most need to persist.

Through that persistence we may develop enough clarity about ourselves and our situation to recognise real truth when we hear it — and to know the difference between it and untruth.

The degree of resistance we experience depends largely on how near we are to inner transformation.

If we are close to recognising and changing one of these inner directives, the unconscious and pre-programmed parts of ourselves are likely to resist strongly. When we are not so near change, the resistance is usually less. This explains why we sometimes experience a great deal of resistance, and other times there is much less. It also explains why it is so important to keep practising right through the resistance.

The real key to recognising resistance is in realising that **any reason you have for not meditating is resistance**, no matter how reasonable it sounds. If you have decided to do it and you don't do it, then some part of you is resisting. It is entirely your choice whether or not to go along with this.

28. Regaining the Path

When we have been caught by our resistance and wandered off the path of our meditation technique, we sometimes respond by becoming angry with ourselves. We often have a basic misunderstanding about our resistance. We may believe it is trying to sabotage us, that it is self-destructive, that it is the enemy within the gates. From the point of view of our conscious minds this may be true; from the viewpoint of another part of ourselves, our resistance is trying to save us from the dangerous and reckless folly of the conscious mind.

There is a very primitive part of ourselves, one of the ancient dragons which lives in deep canyons below the Plain of Reflections. It operates purely on a trial and error basis and on past experience. It attempts to move toward pleasure and to avoid pain. This part of us is not creative, it cannot look to the future, and it cannot imagine alternatives to old behaviours. In a nutshell, its motto seems to be: I did this yesterday and I survived; the only safe thing is to do it again today.

This primitive mind within tries to protect us from all change, especially change that involves transforming ourselves. It doesn't like change in the world, although it knows that is inevitable, but it especially abhors change in ourselves. We need to recognise that *resistance comes from a part of ourselves that is doing its best to help us survive.*

This dragon in the depths has certain programmes or unconscious directives that we have, at some time, accepted as having important survival value. When we try to act against or change these directives, we evoke resistance. The Plain of Resistance was never meant to be a battleground, and there are much better ways of dealing with resistance than by attempting to fight it.

It is very important that, when we become aware that our resistance has led us astray, we avoid becoming impatient or irritated about it. A feeling of calmness and serenity should be a part of the meditative experience, and anything which will work against this is another form of resistance and should be avoided. As we have seen, resistance can come in layers and layers. Patience is essential. Avoid self-criticism, impatience, and other negative and counter-productive activities which disturb the peace of our inner world. When we feel frustration or anger at ourselves or at something in our environment, it often helps to be aware that this is *yet another way* of becoming lost in the woods. What we really need to do is to take a deep, deep breath, consciously letting go of the emotion as we exhale — and go on meditating.

29. Staying on Track

When we notice that we have wandered off the track, we can simply acknowledge that we are resisting a bit and suggest to ourselves that perhaps this is worth thinking about later on, after we're through practising, but right now is not the time for it. The tone of mental 'voice' should be as patient and kind as the one you would use to a much-loved child. Then the exercise is continued until the preselected time is up.

An even better alternative, is to realise that 'thoughts' can come and go as a background to our meditation. If we keep focused on the practice of our particular technique, these random thoughts can only enter into the 'cracks' in our attentiveness. **We can make use of our resistance by using it to remind ourselves that we could be paying closer attention to our focus.** This is a lovely, tricky turnaround in the mind, a kind of mental judo, and will do more than anything else to discourage our resistance.

The more concentrated our practice is, the fewer interruptions we have. We need not struggle or argue with ourselves at all, but simply use each distraction to remind us to attend to our focus more and more.

There is yet another way of dealing with certain kinds of distraction — by embracing them.

Embracing the Enemy

If we are concentrating on suppressing awareness of something, we are not actually practising our technique. This exercise sidesteps the idea of confrontation by using the various distracting and disturbing noises in our environment as a positive focal point in our meditation, rather than as a distraction that must be fought.

Sit in a comfortable, erect position. Allow yourself to become aware of the movement of your abdomen as you breathe.

Use the natural sounds of your environment as the external focal point. Remain aware of your breathing while you listen carefully, and name each sound as you hear it. For example, you might mentally say: car . . . refrigerator . . . breath . . . voices . . . music . . . voices . . . breath . . . et cetera. The sounds are not to be thought about — just observed and named without a 'good' or 'bad' value being placed upon them.

Allow each sound to take you deeper into the meditative state, no matter what kind of a sound it is.

Throughout the practice time, be constantly aware of the movement of the breath in the lower abdomen.

The eyes may be shut or slightly opened with the gaze lowered.

A frequent 'side-effect' of this kind of exercise is that it reprogrammes our response to the noises around us and they become neutral or even relaxing, rather than irritating or alarming. Obviously, some noises (the baby crying, someone screaming in pain or fear) are meant to be alarming and do require our attention. However, we respond to many noises that have nothing to do with us with the same alarm reaction. These sounds, which are actually neutral or unimportant, are usually in the majority and real alarms are quite rare. If you have a problem about noise, it's worth giving this technique a try. It usually takes a while just to begin to switch the response, but it is worth persisting. A month or so of daily practice will usually make a radical and lasting change.

In the same spirit of embracing the 'enemy' within the gates, we can sometimes use physical pain as a focal point for our meditation. The technique is very simple.

Sit comfortably erect, close your eyes, and become aware of your breathing. Take time to allow your breath to become relaxed and to flow freely and deeply.

When your breath has become quiet and soft, allow yourself to become aware of the area around your heart. Imagine that your heart is radiating warmth and that this gentle heat warms your breath as you inhale. The air you exhale is warmer than the air you inhale — imagine that it is this warmth around your heart that makes it so.

When you are able to imagine that heart warmth in each breath, begin to imagine that as you exhale, your breath goes out and simultaneously the warmth goes to the area of the pain. Imagine the warmth softening the area around the pain.

Don't try to do anything with the pain itself — just rest your awareness on the area around it and imagine it softening and letting go with each warm breath. Continue to do this until you feel that this area has become as warm and as soft as it can at this time. If you lose your concentration, first re-establish the warm breath and then return to the softening.

When you feel that you have completed all the warming and softening around the pain that you can do at this time, just allow the warmth to flow into the centre of the pain itself while you return your attention to the warmth in your heart.

You don't need to think about this inward flow or try to do anything with it — in fact, it's best if you don't. Just hold the thought for a fleeting moment that this is happening, and shift your awareness back to the breath and the warmth in the heart.

Imagine the warmth of the heart radiating downward, through your body and legs and feet. Imagine it radiating outward, through your shoulders and arms and hands. Imagine it radiating upward, through your neck and head. Take your time over this and allow yourself to really imagine each part of it clearly.

Now take a couple of deep breaths, open your eyes, flex your fingers and toes, and if you like, stretch.

Some people find this kind of exercise wonderfully relaxing, and it often seems to reduce or even eliminate pain. Partly, this is because our natural tendency is to tense up around a pain to brace the area and protect it from further damage. Unfortunately, this tension actually increases the sensation of pain. If we can release the tension, the pain is often dramatically reduced, and this exercise is a gentle, non-confrontive way of doing this.

We have spent a great deal of time thinking about our resistance and how to turn the whole thing on its head and use it to our best advantage in our practice. Only by understanding and consciously working with our resistance will we actually make meditation a part of our daily lives. And of course, it helps if we can be relaxed about the whole thing.

Part V

On Letting Go

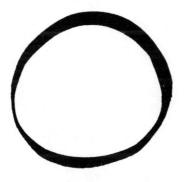

30. Why Are We Hurrying So Fast?

On our way through life, we often seem to forget that we should be enjoying and savoring the journey. The same is true of travelling through our inner world — we need to be relaxed to gain the full benefit of being there. Relaxation techniques are not quite the same as meditation, but they are similar, and they may be helpful to you in getting the most out of your meditation practice.

Any one who has ever 'tried to relax' when tense or upset knows that the phrase 'simple relaxation' is a bit of a joke — relaxation is not so simple when we most need it. And our attitude toward life is significantly expressed in the phrase 'try to relax'. Relaxing is not something we can do by *trying* — it is something we can only do by *allowing* it to happen.

Relaxation is not an active process; tension is the active part. We actually have to work at being tense. Tension is one muscle (or group of muscles) trying to do something, and other muscles trying to stop it from happening. Tension echoes back and forth in our bodies, forming patterns of discomfort and stress. Our feelings say 'do', our minds say 'don't', and our bodies get caught in between, trying to respond to both sets of commands, like a child with arguing parents. To relax, all we need to do is to stop holding the tension, to stop working at it, to let go.

One of the benefits of meditation is that, because our attention is on something other than the thoughts or feelings that usually maintain the state of tension, and because our feelings and thoughts are in harmony, relaxation just naturally happens. There are no messages going from the mind to the body, telling it to maintain the stress. Bodies are generally sensible — they only maintain tension when they are being told to or when they have been told to so many times over so long a period that they have forgotten how to let go.

There are important differences between relaxation and meditation, and this is one of them. In our meditation, some relaxation — often quite a lot — occurs naturally, but in using a relaxation technique, letting go is the whole of our intention. We meditate sitting up, with our spines erect, because this helps us to maintain our alertness, but we often do relaxation techniques lying down so we can really let go of all the muscles.

Somehow, it seems that relaxation ought to be easy if it is just letting go. However, we often have such habitual tension that the muscles have actually forgotten how to release and have to relearn. Most of us have some muscular tensions that are always there, whether they serve any useful purpose or not.

Many people, for example, are surprised to learn the the muscles on top of the shoulders should be as soft as any other relaxed muscle — they definitely should not be hard and lumpy. Much of the time they really are needed only to hold up our shirts or dresses — and this is not a job that requires nearly as much muscle power as we seem to put into it. There are muscles in the jaw and others along the spine which many people consistently hold in tension. And then many of us have our own individual selection of muscles which are virtually never allowed to relax.

Very few people have any idea of how to let go, especially how to relax the muscle groups where there is habitual tension. Meditation will nearly always result in good physical relaxation in time, but many of us can enhance the benefits we gain from meditation by learning to relax thoroughly.

31. Stopping for a While

So how do we stop? How can we just let go when we have forgotten what true relaxation feels like? The two techniques described below are commonly used for relaxation therapy and are very beneficial if practised regularly. People often find that doing an abbreviated version of one of these relaxation techniques prior to their meditation practice helps them to concentrate more fully on the chosen exercise. Both of these relaxation techniques, unlike the meditative exercises themselves, are best done while lying on your back on a firm, comfortable surface or sitting upright in a comfortable chair with your back supported. Clothing should be loose and comfortable.

Progressive Relaxation

The more active of the two techniques is done by progressively tensing and then relaxing muscle groups. Starting with the feet, first on one side and then on the other, work up through the calves, the knees, the thighs, the buttocks, the upper back, the abdomen, the chest, the hands, the forearms, the upper arms, the shoulders, the neck, the face, and the scalp. Each muscle group is tensed tightly and then relaxed. Do first the right side, then the left while working through the feet, legs, buttocks, hands, arms and shoulders.

Some people may find it beneficial to do the entire exercise three times in succession, gaining deeper levels of relaxation each time.

When you have gone through the entire body in this way, just allow yourself to lie in place, remaining relaxed for a quarter of an hour or so, not trying to do or think of anything. After that is a good time to practise your meditation technique.

Caution: If you have health problems, consult your doctor before trying to do this exercise as it is fairly strenuous. If in doubt, use the following relaxation technique instead.

Autogenic Training

This second technique is a more passive type of relaxation. In this exercise, the same sequence is followed as in the progressive relaxation, starting at the feet and going up to the scalp, but the muscles are not tensed. Instead, slowly repeat three times: my right foot is warm and heavy. *Do not try to force anything to happen; just allow relaxation to take place.*

Pay particular attention to the muscles of the face, be especially aware of

*relaxing the jaw, the lips, the tongue, the eyes, the upper and lower eyelids, and
the muscles of the forehead.*

*If you do not like to use the words 'heavy' or 'warm' for some reason, you could
use another word such as 'floating' or 'tingling' or 'quiet'. Words such as 'relaxed'
or 'comfortable' should be avoided if you think your body may be conditioned to
argue with or to resist them.*

This exercise may be repeated as needed, allowing a deeper level of
relaxation each time.

32. A Quiet Place

Once we have learned to slow down, there is something else we can do
to enhance the relaxation process. This is a Yoga relaxation exercise
(sometimes called *Yoga of the Small Exit)* which includes the progressive
relaxation technique. You begin by using the progressive relaxation
exercise (although the autogenic training exercise could be used instead,
if it suits you better). When the cycle of the exercise has been completed,
a mental exercise is done while the body is relaxed. The mental exercise
consists of imagining a beautiful and restful place into being around
yourself.

This resting place is to be thought of as being created around you, not
as a place to which you go. The difference is that imagining going
somewhere takes you away from where you really are, while imagining
that where you are is a lovely, restful place carries over into your daily life
and changes your perception of and emotional response to your
surroundings.

*After going through the relaxation process once, build a complete scene around
yourself. For example, you might wish to imagine yourself lying in the sunshine,
surrounded by grass. That is not a sufficient description. How deep is the grass?
Are there flowers in it? If so, where and what kind? What scent do they have?
What season is it? What time of day? Is there a breeze? If so, how strong? What*

does the grass smell like? Are there other scents? How hard is the ground? What is touching your body? A complete scene is to be built in the mind with details from all of the senses — sight, hearing, smell, taste, and touch.

When this ideal resting place has been constructed, just relax mentally and experience being there. Don't continue to try to imagine it any more thoroughly; just experience the feeling and sensations of being in that special place. You will probably find that each time you practise this exercise, the surroundings become more clear and detailed and vivid in your mind. Imagination improves with practice.

If thoughts are things — and they are — then for this time you have been in this place, which has been specifically designed to be the best place for you to relax in peace and beauty. The yogis maintain that, if your concentration is good and if the place has been sufficiently well constructed and defined, you have really been there — physically as well as mentally. Theoretically, I suppose that with sufficient mental control, you might even be able to get a tan there. This is even cheaper than Morocco, and there is no struggle with crowded and over-scheduled airports.

33. Floating on the Sea, Dissolving on the Sand

Floating is a simple letting-go of things. If your attachment to your body and brain seems a bit loose at the best of times, this is probably not a good thing for you, but if your tendency is to be rigid or over-controlled or tense, perhaps emotionally repressed, this technique might be quite helpful.

Lie down and just let go of your muscles, your body, your bones, your thoughts, your feelings. You don't do anything. Every time you become aware of something, just relinquish it from your mind and body as you breathe out. This is not a relaxation technique nor a meditative exercise — they are disciplines, an exercising, if you will, of our mental and spiritual 'muscles'. This is just becoming totally limp, without boundaries, gently awake and gently aware.

It is sometimes possible to sink very deeply into this quite rapidly, but other times it may be more difficult. Often it helps to do a meditative or relaxing exercise first. Many people also find certain kinds of quiet, flowing music helpful.

The feeling this process leads to is similar to the letting-go that happens in meditation or relaxation, but definitely not the same, and it seems to be a complement to (but certainly not a substitute for) meditation and relaxation techniques.

There is a related technique, which we might call *dissolving*.

You simply lie on the earth and let yourself dissolve into it, letting yourself experience being a part of the earth. Don't make any effort to do this — just let it happen.

This is a relaxing-into, a kind of surrendering. It differs from *floating* in that *dissolving* is a melding, a becoming one with something else, something large and serene, while floating is more of a being nothing.

All of these things — *floating, dissolving, meditating* — have certain similar effects: a sense of serenity and deep peace, a recharging of energy, a sense of having thoroughly rested. This is, of course, accompanied by the obvious things of reduced physiological stress, a more balanced response to the circumstances of life, et cetera. Yet each of these techniques has different results as well.

Meditation strengthens certain abilities — self healing, concentration, attainment of mental skills. It seems primarily a mental-energetic activity which, of course, affects all of one's being.

Dissolving nourishes us in some hard-to-define way. When we have done it and really sunk into the earth, we feel cherished, nurtured, and strengthened. We usually feel 'plugged in' to something very large and powerful and loving. Our response to it seems primarily emotional with physical and mental 'side effects'.

The effect of *floating* is harder to define. The response seems primarily spiritual/emotional — there is a sense of lightness and a kind of pervasive, free-floating joy. Something people often notice is that they feel they have shed burdens on some deeply unconscious level, burdens they didn't know they were carrying. It seems to ease transformation.

Relaxation is quite difficult for some of us because it is about letting go and releasing boundaries and trusting — and for many of us, that is the hardest thing to do. We may have a lot of fears and insecurities that arise from being ungrounded and uncentered, and we need to learn to deal with those in a positive way.

Part VI

On Monsters & Reality

34. Mirages & Illusions

On many ancient maps there were places marked with comments like 'Dragons Be Here' and 'Monsters Abideth In This Place'. Cartographers, like most people, are suspicious of the unknown and populate it with illusory monsters. In most spiritual traditions it is assumed that the great majority of people sleepwalk through life, about half (or even less) aware of what is really going on in the world and in themselves. We live, according to that view, in a dream world — and sometimes the dream becomes a nightmare and gallops off with us. Some, or even a great deal, of what we perceive as 'reality' is in fact our fantasies and projections, our mirages and illusions.

Much of modern psychological thought agrees with this. Our mental Plain of Reflections reflects the outside world as seen through ourselves — through our attitudes, our beliefs, our fears, our desires — and everything we see on that plain is, to some extent, coloured and shaped by us.

We see imaginary monsters and mirages of happiness — and while we are looking at them we are apt to miss whatever real joys and dangers are out there. Much of the time objective reality is obscured by an inner and subjective view, as if shrouded in a fog of faulty perceptions caused by our emotional responses to life. This is why meditation is frequently spoken of as leading to an 'awakening' or an 'illumination'.

Far more often than most of us realise, we live in a world that is partly real, partly projected emotions or fears, and partly wishful thinking. Children do this less; it is something we learn to do as we get older. Children are very matter-of-fact, taking things as they come, however unpleasant. When things are bad, they suffer, and when things get better, they 'return to centre' and are happy. A small child spends very little time dreading what might happen or regretting what did or didn't happen. They live in the present, and if they are not in pain or difficulty at the moment, they are content or even happy.

Adults, on the other hand, have learned to live more in the future and the past, in our mirages and illusions about what might happen, what ought to happen, and what did happen but, we think, shouldn't have. We tend to live in this stuff in our heads instead of in what Is.

Over a period of time the practice of meditation exercises helps to clear away some of the fog and dispel the mirages and illusions. There are other techniques, similar to meditation, which are specifically designed to help create mental and emotional clarity. We call these 'grounding' or 'earthing' exercises because they bring us out of our fantasies and emotions and back to the real world. In the next chapters we will be talking a lot about being 'grounded' or 'earthed' and 'centered' and about just what that means, but first let's take a quick look at the attitudes which cause us to become ungrounded and off-centre.

35. Chasing Mirages and Falling in Pits

There are several possible holes in consciousness through which we fall out of reality and into our own fantasies. Let's look at a few of the most common.

A Case of Mistaken Identity

One of the most frequent pitfalls is when we become so deeply involved with something that we mistake it for ourselves. This 'something' may be a feeling or a belief or an object.

For example, A is so enthralled by his new washing machine that when someone carelessly scratches it, he reacts as if they had scarred his body. Miss Careless drops the vase B inherited from her great-grandmother and

B completely loses control of herself and explodes in rage. C loses everything on the stockmarket and considers suicide a realistic option. D's lover is unhappy about something at work, so to prove how loyal and how much a part of her he is, D becomes desperately worried and concerned. E takes it as a personal insult when someone doesn't agree with her political views.

In each ease the person has projected their own sense of identity and need for security to someone or something else. They have become centered in that something else, rather than in themselves. These things happen when we forget that we have our own being-in-the-world and we think that externals, like money or objects, or intangibles, like ideals, create our happiness and are essential to our well-being. This sort of thing happens to many people who embark upon some sort of a crusade in which they passionately believe. They may lose all sense of proportion and balance, becoming ungrounded and off-centre.

Control & Manipulation

Another frequently encountered pitfall occurs when we try to control something we cannot control. This uncontrollable something might be other people's feelings, beliefs, and attitudes, or it might be certain situations that are essentially out of our control.

We become ungrounded when we are trying to protect, control, own, or fix something or someone in our environment over which we have no control. We often have the delusion that we can *make* others happy, that we can *make* them want to stop drinking, that we can *fix* their 'bad' habits or attitudes. We may believe that we can control their behaviour and that they have no choice about their response to us and our manipulations. This is an illusion, and we cling to it to protect ourselves from the terrible and frightening truth that we are not in control of the world.

We become ungrounded by trying to pretend that we do have such control — if we can just find the right buttons to push. We become off-centre by becoming so involved in others that we are centered in them instead of in ourselves. This illusion is also used to protect ourselves from the terrible truth that, although we are not in control of the world, we are in control of and responsible for ourselves.

We are operating under a logical fallacy here. It goes something like:

Assumption 1: I can control you — because I'm stronger/smarter than you.

Assumption 2: People who are stronger/smarter than I can control me.

Conclusion: Therefore, I am responsible for your behaviour and feelings, and others are responsible for mine.

The basic flaw in this logic is that neither assumption is true. The old saying that 'you can lead a horse to water, but you can't make him drink' is relevant here. We can push other people's buttons, but they still have choice about their response. If we cannot acknowledge and accept that, we become very confused, often deciding that we are the victims of a malign fate.

The important thing here is that we are not taking responsibility for ourselves — for our thoughts, for our attitudes, for our actions. We may have programmes in our heads that have been adopted from others, and those others may have put a lot of effort into getting us to accept these programmes. In fact, they may have put a lot of pressure on us. However, we still have choice. No matter how deeply a programme is embedded, no matter how strong a habit is, we still have choice. Exercising that choice in a new way may not be easy, it may be incredibly difficult — we may have to try again and again, and we may even need the help of others to break out of the old pattern. But the choice is always ours.

When we are trying to perfect and control our environment instead of ourselves, we are hiding from the truth that the only thing we really have full authority over and responsibility for is ourselves.

Purchasing Approval

Another cause of becoming uncentered is the desire to gain the approval — and with that, we hope, the love — of others.

This is another way of trying to control others. We may feel that, if we do everything the other wants, they *must* approve of and love us. Then they will take care of our needs. To get this, we must become centred in their desires instead of our own, and we make the choices we think they want.

This behaviour pattern has a number of problems. We may not actually be doing what the other wants, and in that case, they may just be annoyed by our efforts and attentions. Or we may be doing what they want and this may just cause them to have contempt for us for having so little self-respect. Or we may do what they want and they hardly notice, taking our efforts for granted. Or, worst of all, we may do what they want and they give us love-on-approval for it. Then we have to keep doing what they want forever and ever and never even think about what we desire, or we will lose that 'love'.

On the subject of love, St. Paul wrote:

> Love is patient and kind; love is not jealous or boastful; it is not arrogant or rude. Love does not insist on its own way; it is not irritable or resentful; it does not rejoice at wrong, but rejoices in the right. Love bears all things, believes all things, hopes all things, endures all things. [5]

He didn't use the now-fashionable words 'unconditional love', but he was obviously saying exactly that.

The biggest problem about love-on-approval is that, in order to please others, our own feelings and desires are often suppressed and ignored. This is potentially harmful to our health. Emotional energy has to go somewhere. If our feelings are ignored and repressed, they still exist as an energy within us. If they are strong enough or recur often enough, they eventually assume a destructive life of their own, either causing us to sabotage ourselves by behaviour that doesn't get the desired reaction or by creating illness in our bodies — or both. It is now widely recognised that the stress generated by this kind of behaviour and the emotions that go with it can be a contributing factor in cancer and other diseases [6].

Sensitivity

Yet another problem that causes us to lose our balance is when we are more sensitive to and aware of others than we are earthed and centered in ourselves.

This again is related to, but not quite the same as the ideas above. This kind of sensitivity is called 'empathy' and can be very useful if recognised and properly channelled. It is a valuable trait for anyone who works in a capacity where they need to truly understand others. In fact, it is a valuable trait in all human relationships. More widespread empathy would radically improve our social and political structures. However, empathy is a two-edged sword.

Some people seem to be empathic from early childhood. In an effort to protect themselves from the discomfort of others, they grow up learning to please others first and themselves last. There are reasons for doing this. First, if we have that kind of empathy, we hurt when others hurt, and we will do whatever is required to make the pain go away. Second, there may also be the belief that, if we make others happy, they will be kind to us and make us happy — or at least not hurt us so much.

This is the same kind of thing as the set of assumptions above, in that it relegates control of our emotions to others. Unfortunately (or fortunately), giving others what they think they want does not always make them happy. In fact, it usually results in them thinking that they need Something More or Something Else in order to be happy, so we have to keep trying — because, somehow, making them happy will make things all right for us, we hope.

When our feelings are muddled with the feelings of those around us, we may be confused about what is happening to us and what is happening to someone else. We may become susceptible to the inner turmoil and distress of others, and their emotion throws us off-centre just as certainly as our own does. As we work with becoming sensitive to our own inner selves, we also tend to become more sensitive to the energies of others and to our environment. Our capacity to experience empathy, to share the feelings of others, increases, and while both awareness and sensitivity are useful tools, they need skill in use, like all tools. When our sensitivity is in charge of us instead of the other way around, we are off-centre.

Denial

Another common way in which we fall out of reality into a pit of our own making is when we try to convince ourselves that something is true when it is false, or false when it is true.

We tend to become unearthed and uncentered whenever life, as we perceive it, becomes difficult and painful or when some extraordinary growth opportunity is presented to us by a loving universe. The first thing many of us do in such circumstances is to curl up in a little tight ball in our solar plexus and start saying things like 'I know you didn't really mean that' or 'surely it's all a mistake' or 'I'm certain you must be wrong' or 'that can't possibly be true'. We become ungrounded and try to live in our fantasies instead of the real world.

Runaway Emotions

Another way in which we lose contact with reality is when we stop thinking and let our emotions have free reign.

We may become unearthed by assuming that, because we feel an emotion, this emotion is our only possible response. It owns us instead of us owning it, and we respond blindly from that momentary emotion rather than from the true centre of our beings. If we become angry or fearful, we tend to become so involved with that anger, or fear, that we become centered in our emotions instead of in ourselves. The same thing happens with the objects of our infatuations or our excessive concerns. Whenever we are in any highly emotional state we tend to become ungrounded.

If we have consistently experienced any of these situations and responses listed above over a substantial length of time, we may easily have formed the habit of remaining unearthed, forgetting what it felt like to be really centered in ourselves. We then live our whole lives in a floating soap bubble of unreality.

Why be real, some may ask, when fantasy is more fun?

Alas, fantasy is only more fun *part of the time*. We may happily float in our soap bubble for a while, but sooner or later we will encounter one of reality's sharp corners. If we are ungrounded and uncentered practically to the point of psychosis, we can just pretend it didn't happen. However, for most people, the bursting of their bubble is a painful experience — the amount of pain being directly correlated with how high off the earth we were when our bubble burst.

We become powerless when we are ungrounded. Other people find it relatively easy to push and manipulate us. When we find ourselves doing what they want and not what we want, we are not usually happy about it. We may blame them, accusing them of being pushy and controlling (and they may even be that), but the real fault lies in ourselves. We are the ones who have said 'yes' when we want to say 'no'.

Becoming uncentered and unearthed is quite frustrating, because the very times that we go floating off are the times that we most need to be in our strong place, to be centered, to be down-to-earth, to be objective, to be real. Only then can we see clearly enough to make wise choices.

36. Seeing Clearly

So what can we do in order to become more earthed and centered, to clear the fog and dispel the mirages from our Plain of Reflections? Do you remember ever being told to just take a deep breath and get control of yourself? Let's try it and see what happens.

First, notice how you are feeling at this moment. How do you feel physically? Emotionally? Mentally? Don't try to change anything, but simply notice any tensions or other feelings that may be present.

Next, to see how you are breathing at the moment, place one hand on your chest and one on your abdomen. Notice where your breath flows. Which hand moves the most when you breathe? Does either hand not move at all?

Allow yourself to begin breathing so that the hand on the chest (and the chest itself) holds almost still and the one on the abdomen feels most of the movement of the breath.

Take at least ten breaths this way. Breathe slowly enough so you don't hyperventilate or become dizzy.

After you have done this, continue the same breathing pattern and begin to imagine any unpleasant energy within you (fatigue, tension, nervousness, distraction, et cetera) flowing down through your body and legs, through your feet, and into the earth. Imagine it flowing down as you exhale each breath. Keep being aware of your breath in your abdomen as you do this.

After several minutes of this, go back to just concentrating on your breath and on the movements of your hands, allowing your abdomen to move, but keeping the chest relatively still. Do this for another fifteen breaths.

When you are finished, check once more and see what feelings you are now experiencing.

What did you feel before doing the breathing? After? Do you notice anything now that you didn't notice before — that is, are you any more self-aware? Has anything changed in the way your body or emotions feel?

This simple breathing exercise helps to clear us of tensions or feelings we may be carrying around, but which are not really appropriate to the present moment. We don't consciously need to know what those things are — our unconscious minds know and we only need to give ourselves permission to let them go.

If you have trouble with this simple exercise, I strongly recommend that you practise the earthing and centering exercises in the following chapters until you have a good sense of what it really means to be earthed and centered.

Let's think about what it means to be awake and aware instead of sleepwalking blindly through our lives. Your whole life will improve if you have not been grounded and centered and you become so. Simply being earthed will, in itself, eliminate a lot of problems that presently seem important and that worry you and take up your energy. Many of our problems are simply the result of not seeing clearly, or of not realising that some things are out of our control or are not our responsibility. You might as well get these unreal problems out of your way so you can work on the things that are real and that do need and will benefit from your attention.

The following chapters discuss particular aspects of being centered and earthed and give a variety of exercises to practise. Even if you feel that you are pretty firmly attached to the earth and well in touch with your true self, I still recommend that you try the exercises. We all have our moments of ungroundedness, and these exercises will only work under the pressure of stressful situations if they have been practised in advance. The exercises help us to learn to be more aware of just how earthed or unearthed we are at any given time. We need to form the habit of checking our own sense-of-ourselves for centeredness and connectedness, especially when we are under any kind of stress.

Part VII

On Not Wobbling

37. Keeping Fit for the Journey

Physical fitness is receiving much well-deserved attention these days, but not everyone realises its profound effect upon our explorations of the Plain of Reflections and Sea of Changes — let alone our mountaineering attempts. We can greatly help our meditation practice by being earthed and centered in our physical body.

It is obvious that we can concentrate on meditation better if we are not too tired, too hungry, or in too much discomfort to attend fully to the exercise. It is also obvious that good physical condition makes a positive contribution to whatever we do. Good muscle tone encourages good mental tone. A body that is low in energy goes with a depressed mental state. In addition to those things, posture is much more important than is generally recognised.

It really is important to sit in meditation in an erect yet relaxed position. We need to sit like a mountain or like a strong, old oak, awake, alert, relaxed, and utterly solid. A very few people will be unable, for physical reasons, to sit correctly. If you have this problem, it need not discourage you because you can still benefit in many ways from meditation. However, the rest of us can use our posture as a powerful aid to our practice. Quite apart from the fact that the entire body, including the brain, is designed to work best in an erect, balanced, and relaxed posture, the practice of meditation especially benefits from good posture for a several reasons.

Messages From the Unconscious

One of the reasons that sitting properly is helpful to our practice is that the body and the mind affect each other. Getting the body still and centered helps to get the mind into a similar state. A body that is out of balance, off-centre, or uncomfortable makes a constant demand to 'do something about this' to the mind and encourages anxiety and lack of concentration.

For example, if a person were to sit with his shoulders pulled up and forward and his head drooping, his body would feel as if he were hiding from something, trying not to be seen. Then, unconsciously, his mind would look for threats and dangers to hide from — and when we look for a thing to fear, we can always manage to find something. The next step is that we believe that whatever-it-is-we-have-found is the thing that frightened us in the first place, not realising that we simply frightened ourselves. A centered, balanced body, on the other hand, senses and projects tranquility and well-being.

Our body language says all kinds of things about and to us. It may say that we are angry, that we are exhausted, that we are off-balance, that we are unable to support ourselves, or that we are poised, centered, and balanced. Our habitual posture gives messages to others as well as to ourselves about our personality and our approach to life. Stand in front of a mirror in your usual posture and look at yourself with a stranger's eyes. What sort of a person do you see? Think about the messages your body is giving to you and to others — you may want to change them.

The message your body needs to be giving your mind in meditation is that you are centered and earthed, alert, yet relaxed, focused, yet still — and these same attitudes are also very useful in daily life.

Comfort & Circulation

Another reason for sitting comfortably erect is that physical discomfort interferes with meditation. The habit of poor posture is far more tiring and less comfortable than the habit of good posture, and a body in an unbalanced position quickly becomes tired and painful. Some muscles are stretched and strained, others are cramped and crowded, and circulation is cut off, causing toxins to accumulate in parts of the body, which also lack oxygen and nourishment. Poor posture sabotages many of the physical benefits we would otherwise receive from meditation. It is difficult for a body which is cramped and uncomfortable, starved of oxygen and nourishment, and filled with toxins to experience much in the way of well-being.

Many people have such habitually poor posture that they cannot sit erect comfortably for any length of time. When I first began meditating, no one told me how important posture was and I practised leaning back in a comfortable old chair. A few years later I joined a group that practised Zazen, a sitting meditation which places great emphasis on posture. I very nearly gave it up because I found sitting erect with an unsupported back for an hour to be very painful — in fact, I couldn't do it for more than about ten minutes. I was thought to have fairly good posture, but I soon learned that what had passed for good posture was, in fact, a rigid and out-of-balance back, which became very painful when asked to support itself in stillness for any time.

Making changes in our posture can be very uncomfortable at first, not only physically, but emotionally as well. A new posture asks us to feel differently about ourselves as well as to use our muscles in unaccustomed way. However, improving our posture pays off in so many ways that it is well worth the effort and possible temporary discomfort involved.

We sometimes equate sitting or standing 'up straight' with a kind of pseudo-military attitude (chest out, shoulders back, stomach in, tension between the shoulder blades, in the shoulders, down the arms, and into the hands, tension in the throat and neck, tension in the abdomen, tension in the buttocks and all the way down the legs to the curled toes). There is a very big difference between this and good, balanced posture.

In good posture, little effort is involved, and each part of the body supports the one above it with minimal muscle activity. When our posture is good, we feel well grounded (our centre of gravity is held securely over our feet) and we feel stable, yet flexible — emotionally as well as physically. We need to be really aware of what our bodies are doing and feeling, and in order to do that, we need to understand what being grounded and being ungrounded actually feel like.

One of the worst things about losing our balance is that we are often too unbalanced to realise that the problem is in us rather than in other people or things. The earth has not wobbled, we have. However, there are several symptoms that can indicate that we may not be properly connected to our bodies:

We trip over things, bump into things, and drop things a lot. The worst stage of this is tripping over things that are not there.

We find bruises and can't think how we got them.

The acute stage of physical disease comes as a surprise to us because we have not noticed any of the preliminary warning signs.

We feel tired all the time, and we don't understand why or do anything to correct the situation.

We don't eat, exercise, or rest properly.

Our house, office, room, and/or desk is disorderly.

We get lost and/or we lose things.

We are accident-prone and/or clumsy.

We habitually eat, work, play, drive, and do other things at excessively high speed.

If you recognise any of these signs, you may benefit from the following physical earthing exercises. If any of them make a change in the way you perceive or experience the world, then you will know you have been at least a little out of alignment and somewhat insecurely attached to your body and the earth.

Being physically centered and earthed is the key to developing a sense of security about our physical presence in the world. Let's consider how our posture can be improved in order to help us to do this.

38. Sit Like a Mountain, Stand Like a Pine

Sometimes our posture is so out of balance that the problem is obvious, but more often the imbalances are subtle. The following exercises may help you to be more aware of the importance of subtle tensions and stresses in your own posture. With any luck, they will also help you to find a more balanced stance in the world.

Standing Like a Pine

1. Stand up, your feet about shoulder width apart, your weight evenly balanced on both feet.

Flex your knees slightly.

Put your awareness in the soles of your feet. Notice where your weight is — is it in the toes or the heels?

Let yourself rock slightly and slowly back and forth until you feel your weight balanced right over the centre of your arches. Stop there.

Is this where you usually stand?

Notice the tensions in the muscles of your legs. How much can you let them relax in this position? Is there a way that you can position your legs so that they relax even more and you are even more centered over your arches?

Try walking a few steps and then finding this balance again. Do it several times, until you can find it quickly and easily.

2. Stand up, feet slightly apart, knees slightly flexed, evenly balanced on both feet, and find a centered balance, as in the exercise above.

Feel the soles of your feet and notice whether your weight is over the inside or the outside of your feet.

Rock first your right foot, then your left foot from side to side on the ground, until you feel where the centre between the two sides, inside and outside, of each foot is.

Now let yourself sway slowly and gently from side to side until you have your weight right over the centre of the arch on both sides.

Again, notice the tensions in the muscles of your legs and allow them to relax as much as they can in this position. Is there a way that you can shift your weight over your feet so that your legs relax even more and you are even more centered over your arches?

Practise walking and re-finding your balance, front and back, side to side, until you can find it quickly and easily.

3. Stand up, feet apart, knees slightly flexed, and balance yourself evenly on both feet, with your weight above the arches.

Be aware of the muscles in your abdomen and lower back.

Keeping your feet and legs in the same position, weight over the arches, tilt your pelvis back and forth until you find a balance for it with minimal tension in the abdominal and back muscles.

Let go of the muscles in your back and abdomen. Can you fine tune your position so that the muscles can relax even more?

Check that your balance over your arches is still right — it may require fine adjustment.

Repeat the same process with your rib cage, being aware of the muscles in the upper abdomen and mid back. When your position is right, your chest will open like a flower and it will feel good to take a really deep breath.

Let your shoulders fall.

Check that your balance over your arches is still right — it may require fine adjustment.

Repeat the same process with your head, being aware of the muscles in your neck and throat and between your shoulder blades. Let your throat be open.

Check that your balance over your arches is still right.

Practise walking and re-finding the most centered, balanced position you can, until you can find it easily.

4. Stand up, feet apart, slightly knees flexed, evenly balanced on both feet, and find a centered balance, as in the exercise above.

Imagine that the sun is right above you, and its light lifts you upward. Imagine that light going through the centre of your body, holding it aligned and in balance.

Imagine that the earth is supporting your feet and that you feel that support all the way up through your body, lifting every bone, every muscle, every cell. Let yourself imagine and feel the sensation of being held and lifted.

Imagine that there are roots between you and the earth. Perhaps you cannot tell if they are the earth's roots in you, or your roots in the earth. It doesn't matter which — it only matters that you and the earth are securely connected — and strength flows from the earth to you.

You are like a tall, straight pine, deeply rooted, supported by the earth, energised by the sun.

5. Stand like a pine. Now, practise walking and moving like a pine moving in the wind.

Now we are going to try a similar thing while sitting down.

Sitting Like a Mountain

1. Sit in a hard (or at least, very firm) chair or cross-legged on the floor if this is comfortable. You may need to use a cushion to lift your feet (in a chair) or to sit on (on the floor) so that your legs and back are more comfortable. Sit forward on the chair so that your back is a few inches from the back of the chair. You will need some space to lean back and forth. Your feet need to rest comfortably flat on the floor, without the circulation being cut off in the back of your legs by the edge of the chair. If the chair is too high for this, put a cushion or some books under your feet so that your legs will be comfortable.

Be aware of the feel of the bones of the pelvis on the seat of the chair. Lean slightly forward and back a few times to get the feel of this.

Now, be aware of the muscles of your abdomen as you rock slightly forward and back. Notice that as you move back beyond the midpoint, your abdominal muscles start to tighten up. You may also notice the muscles of your thighs tighten slightly.

Next, practise noticing the muscles in your lower and middle back as you rock back and forth, very slowly and gently. Notice how they start to tense as soon as you lean forward past the centre balance point.

Find the centre balance point, so that neither the abdominal nor the back muscles are tensing, not even the slightest bit, and your weight is balanced right over the pelvic bones where they press on the chair.

Imagine your pelvis being like the base of a mountain, resting on the earth.

Rise from the chair and walk about a bit, then go back and try it again. Do this several times, until you feel that you have just the right balance and can find it again easily.

2. Again, let your pelvis rest on the chair like a mountain rests on the earth, balanced over the point of contact between the chair and your pelvic bones, feeling the relaxed muscles in your abdomen and back.

Be aware of the sensations in your abdomen and chest. Do they feel cramped or open? Is your body collapsed around your solar plexus? Do you need to move your upper body in order to take a really deep breath down into the abdomen?

Find a position for your rib cage that gives your abdomen and chest a lovely open feeling and which allows you to take deep, deep breaths, all the way to your toes.

Check your balance over your pelvic bones — it may need a slight adjustment to allow for the changed position of your upper body.

Practise a few deep breaths, breathing all the way down through your body, imagining that your breath is travelling clear down to the tips of your toes and back up again.

Feel yourself sitting like a mountain, soaring into the sky, resting solidly on the earth.

Rise from the chair and walk about a bit, then go back and try it again. Do this several times, until you feel that you have just the right balance and can find it again easily.

3. *Again, sit like a mountain, balanced over the point of contact between the chair and your pelvic bones, feeling the relaxed muscles in your abdomen and back. Let your chest and abdomen open, so that your rib cage is balanced on your spine effortlessly. The mountain soars to the sky effortlessly.*

Notice your shoulders. Where are they? What are they doing up there?

Tell your shoulders that all they need to do is to hold up your clothing. If they are holding anything else, ask them to please let go of it.

Check your balance over your pelvic bones and make any adjustments needed.

Move your head from side to side, front to back. Find the position where it is most centered. Let your head float like a cloud above your body. Be aware of the muscles of your neck and throat. If there is any tension there, let it go.

Check your balance over your pelvic bones and make any adjustments needed.

Be a mountain, resting on the earth, soaring to the sky. Let your head float like a cloud. Breathe deeply, down into the roots of the mountain.

Rise from the chair and walk about a bit, then go back and try it again. Do this several times, until you feel that you have just the right balance and can find it again easily.

4. *Sit like a mountain, resting on the earth, soaring into the sky. Let your head float like a cloud.*

Now, be aware of your throat. Is it open or cramped? Sing a loud note. Is there any way you can hold your head and neck so that the note becomes louder and more free?

Let your jaw loose.

Take a deep breath into your pelvis, and sing another loud note, letting it rise

up from the pelvis, unobstructed, through your open chest and throat. Sing your
note from the roots of the mountain.
  Sit like a mountain.
  Breathe.

You can use this technique to balance properly seated either on a chair,
on the floor, or on a low cushion, but it may be helpful to practise it first
in a chair.

In addition to the other reasons we have mentioned for having good
posture in meditation, there are certain physiological processes involving
the brain, spine, and nervous system, which are triggered by the
rhythmic breathing, slowed heart rate, and other phenomena that occur
as we meditate. Itzhak Bentov, a designer and builder of medical
equipment for hospitals and research facilities, became interested in
measuring some of the unusual physiological changes that go on during
meditation.

In his research he became convinced that meditation continued over a
period of time does cause physical changes, including a change in the
mode of functioning of the nervous system. Without getting too
technical, it appears that a rhythmic micro-motion of the body develops
when in deep meditation, and this affects the brain and nervous system.
This movement begins in the chest with a standing wave pattern
generated in the aorta. The standing wave is echoed in the abdomen and
pelvis and by the brain in the skull through a process called 'rhythm
entrainment'. When this motion is fully established, the meditative state
becomes very stable and deepens, enhancing its effect on the cerebro-
spinal nervous system. Bentov writes:

> When a fetus develops in the womb, it undergoes changes which
> mirror human evolution from a fish through the amphibian to the
> mammal. But our findings suggest that this evolution very probably
> has not come to a halt with the way our present nervous system is
> presently functioning. The hidden potential of our nervous system
> may be vast. The mechanism outlined above describes a possible next
> step in the evolution of the nervous system, which can be accelerated
> by the use of certain techniques. [7]

The techniques Bentov has in mind are meditation exercises. The process he describes is believed by some to be the necessary physiological accompaniment to extremely deep relaxation in meditation, where healing of body, psyche, and spirit may most effectively take place, and where we may sometimes experience the ecstasy of the mystic. These processes take place much more effectively when the spine is erect; I do not know whether or not they take place at all in slumped or otherwise poor posture — they are certainly handicapped.

Getting Help

If the old bad habits have become deeply engrained, you would probably find *Hatha Yoga* (the practice of physical stretches and postures) quite helpful, especially in stretching out, strengthening, and straightening the muscles supporting the spine. Some of the postural therapies, such as the Alexander Technique, Feldenkrais, or Callanetics, could also be of great value, especially if you find it difficult to do the exercises given here on your own.

If you are so disconnected from your body that you felt unable to do the exercises above, please do get some skilled help.

Lying Down

We have discussed the reasons for sitting up in correct posture while practising, but sometimes we just can't. We might be injured, we might be too ill, or we might be bedfast for some other reason, but we can still do our meditation techniques. It is a bit harder because we all have a programme in our minds that says: horizontal position + closed eyes + relaxation = sleep. Most of us have been doing that for years and years, and it is a deeply ingrained habit. We are actually supposed to be more than merely awake when we are practising — we are supposed to be alert and intently focused. To be 'not quite asleep' is not good enough. This kind of alertness is really difficult to maintain when we are lying down, and to do so will require special effort.

The important thing in meditating while lying down (besides staying awake long enough to do it) is to keep the spine as nearly as possible in the natural curves it assumes when properly erect. Of course, this must be done within the comfortable bounds of whatever physical problems may exist. Getting the spine reasonably aligned is probably easiest to do if you are lying on your back, when that is possible. If the lower back is uncomfortable when lying flat, a thick pillow under the knees often eases it greatly.

If a person is not injured or bedfast, meditation should be done whenever possible while sitting in a good posture. Apart from the reasons already given, it is not good to programme ourselves to feel that we can practise only lying down or only in complete silence or only in certain surroundings, thus creating unnecessary limitations for ourselves. It is far more useful to become accustomed to meditating in a variety of places and under different circumstances. If I couldn't meditate in airports, airplanes, and trains, life would be a lot more stressful.

Meditative Motion

This is not a substitute for sitting meditation, but simply some ideas which can be applied in daily life to help promote a meditative, clear, and peaceful state of mind in all of our activities. This is an aspect of something that the Buddhists call 'mindfulness'. To be mindful means to be awake and aware all the time, it means to really attend to what you are doing, without your mind being in one place and your body in another. There is a Zen poem that says:

When you are walking,
just walk.
When you are sitting,
just sit.
Above all, don't wobble.

Many of our routine tasks could be done while maintaining a meditative state of mind. We tend to do these things with our minds miles away, busy on unrelated things — often mere mental fussing. The next time you are washing the dishes or the car, sweeping the floor, brushing your teeth, or weeding the garden, allow yourself to fall into rhythmic movements and a meditative state of mind. The dishes get done just as fast, possibly even faster, and with less fatigue when you are aware of the beauty of the soap bubbles, enjoying the feel of your hands in the water, fully present and resting into the rhythm of the moment. Allow the rhythm of the task to hold the whole of your mind.

Finding your natural rhythm, your appropriate pace, is the key to this. If this pace is really connected to a meditative state of mind, it will not be hurried or abrupt or jerky. It will flow naturally from one movement to another. Once we have found and maintained this pace for a while, we are usually astonished at how much we have accomplished and at how little it has tired us. In fact, we may find that, although our body may be pleasantly tired if we have been working for a long time, our minds feel refreshed and alert and clear.

Dancing in a simple, repetitive movement to gentle music can also use the movement of your body to slow down and concentrate your mind. Some exercises, such as T'ai Chi and Yoga are specifically to be practised in a calm, meditative state.

The next time you go for a walk, feel the soles of your feet as you go. Be aware of the sensation of the air where it touches you. Be aware of the things you pass. Be fully in the present moment. This sounds easy — children do it much of the time — but it may be much more difficult than you think. The following exercise may help you to work on it.

'Walking Meditation' Exercise

This is actually a pretty demanding technique, and it is usually done by people with a fair bit of experience. However, you might find it interesting to try, whatever your level.

For the first five minutes, concentrate on being fully aware of the movement of your body — the placement of your feet on the earth, the movement of your legs, your torso, your shoulders and arms, the carriage of your neck and head. Your pace should be slow and deliberate, but not so slow that you wobble.

Still maintaining that self-awareness, spend the next five minutes carefully noticing everything you see below the level of your knees. Don't think about it or about what it all means. Especially, don't get all philosophical about it; just note what is there, be aware of its presence.

The next five minutes is spent, still with full self-awareness, noticing everything between the level of your knees and shoulders. And the following five minutes, continuing in full self-awareness, is spent noticing everything above your shoulders.

For the last five minutes, go back to giving your full attention to your own body and movements.

All of these things give us practice in living and moving in our ordinary world in a calm, relaxed, centered, and earthed state rather than our all-too-often tense and anxious state. We are changing our way of being in the world. The interesting thing is that we get tense because we are trying hard, and we actually do most things better if we are relaxed and alert rather than tense and strained.

We have spent a lot of time on the physical aspects of earthing and centering. This aspect of meditation technique is much neglected by many instructions for meditative exercises, yet it is one of the simplest things we can do to really improve the effectiveness of our practice. The mind and the body are inextricably interconnected, and a floppy body encourages — almost demands — a floppy mind, as a rigid body encourages a rigid mind. Poor posture in our practice is one of the subtle tactics our resistance uses to sabotage us — without us even realising it. It is well worth going through whatever you need to do in the way of stretching and loosening and realigning your body. Posture is a way of encouraging a state of relaxed alertness in ourselves at all times. Not only your meditation, but your whole life will improve.

There are still our thoughts and emotions to be considered in this idea of being earthed and centered, of course, but having the physical body well aligned and in balance gets us poised for a good start.

Part VIII

On Wild Weather & Rough Seas

39. Thunder & Lightning

The Plain of Reflections reflects everything that goes on in our inner world, and one of the things that there usually seems to be a lot of is noise. We babble to ourselves a lot. Sometimes we even roar and thunder. Much of this is habit, but it is a very persistent habit.

One reason that we don't stop the babble is that we have forgotten the value and joy of silence in our own minds. Another is that we have become so accustomed to the noise that we don't realise that our minds could be any different — it's like not hearing the hum of the refrigerator until it goes off and we notice the silence. We talk about 'noise pollution' in our cities and the effects of noise as a stressor for people at work, but we don't seem to notice that the noisiest place in the world is often the inside of our heads. In addition to the thunder rumbling away in our minds, there is the lightning as well. One idea, then another idea, then still another may shoot off in our minds like fireworks or flashes of lightning, dazzling and confusing us. We often don't even really think about the ideas, we just sort of fizz mentally.

When we have become so accustomed to these mental electrical storms that we don't even notice them anymore, how do we know when they are disrupting communications on the Plain of Reflections? Or how do we know that things have become so foggy that we can't see, if we are used to being blind? There are a number of symptoms which indicate that our mental circuits have become scrambled — the real difficulty is in remembering to look for them. Some of these reminders are:

We are absent minded — can't remember where we have put things, what we were doing, or what comes next.

We are vague and easily confused.

We have a lot of silly ideas.

We continually start things and don't finish them. Few or none of our projects are completed because we have started something else.

We are frequently surprised by the consequences of our behaviour.

Other people are often angry or impatient with us, and we don't understand why.

We feel that no one understands us — and this is often true.

We are often muddled about the date, the time, or the place.

Our minds get stuck in a groove, running the same track over and over.

We have really good ideas, but we can't remember what they were.

We are just sure we know what we are doing and everyone else has it wrong.

Our thoughts get set on 'endless replay' and go round and round.

We work on a lot of projects simultaneously and inefficiently.

We spend more time thinking about the future or the past than we do in giving our full attention to the present.

We fail to keep our promises.

We do not take responsibility for our own actions and their consequences.

We generalise a lot: women are . . . , politicians are . . . , old people are . . . , Orientals are . . . Generalisations of this nature are logically invalid, but we use them to avoid observing and trying to understand the real world.

We spend so much time in fantasy that we get little accomplished in the real world.

40. Stilling the Thunder

When we have become lost in trackless forests of confusion and the thunder is rumbling away overhead, we may feel that we need a rescue team. On the Plain of Reflections, the only rescue team available has to come from ourselves. When you originally began doing meditative exercises, probably the first thing you noticed was how difficult it was to keep from thinking of other things. There are, however, several ways to bring the chatterbox in your mind to a halt, at least temporarily. One of the simplest is to hold your breath.

Try taking a deep breath and holding it for a few moments. As you do, notice how easy it is to keep your mind still at the same time. It isn't long before it starts to chatter again, but there is a definite silence to start with. When we have our attention on something else, especially something physical, like our breath, our minds tend to be more quiet. The following exercise uses that principle and it also uses the principle that we can change our internal state simply by being quiet and giving ourselves permission to change.

Breathing In Truth

'Breathing In Truth, Breathing Out Not-Truth' is exactly what the name says.

We simply concentrate on our breath, inhaling while thinking, 'I am breathing in truth' and exhaling with, 'I am breathing out not-truth'. If we imagine 'truth' as an energy and 'not-truth' as a different energy, we can just imagine ourselves filling with one while we empty out the other. We do not think about what the 'truth' or the 'not-truth' specifically are — the inner/higher/wiser Self will take care of that.

This is an exercise that I specifically use when I am stirred up about something and cannot settle down — whether into meditation or anything else. At first it seems easy to keep our awareness focused on our breath, then it often begins to seem boring and pointless (the first sneaky manifestation of resistance). Next the physical discomforts and distractions begin — the itching toe, the aching back, the cramp in the leg. If the inner resistance does not succeed in taking us from the exercise with those, it pulls out its big guns and starts firing bright ideas or distressing thoughts through the conscious mind. This is all just a part of the process: 'not-truth' is resisting letting go. We need to simply keep coming back to 'I am breathing in truth, I am breathing out not-truth' until all the resistance disappears.

Eventually, the resistance does disappear and we find ourselves in a state of complete serenity, a kind of joyful yet quiet balance, a feeling of resting into trust. When I first learned this exercise, that was where I always stopped, thinking I had 'done it' — had reached a proper frame of mind. Later on I realised that I was only then ready to *begin* to practise my meditative technique!

There is another way of helping to earth and centre ourselves with which you might like to experiment. The following is an imagery exercise that many people find very helpful.

You might find it useful to put this exercise on a tape so you can concentrate on the exercise itself, rather than on what comes next. If you do tape it, try to keep your voice soothing and gentle throughout and the pace slow. It need not be exaggeratedly so, and the best way to keep a slow pace is to make frequent pauses in appropriate places, rather than speaking the words very slowly.

Line of Light

Start by taking a few deep breaths, allowing yourself to settle into relaxation as you exhale, becoming just as relaxed as is comfortable for you at this time.

There is an energy centre just below and forward of the base of your spine. Please focus your awareness in that centre. This is the root centre. You may be able to feel or to sense the energy in that centre in some way, perhaps as tingling or warmth or some other sensation, or perhaps you won't — it doesn't matter, just be aware that it is there and focus your attention in that part of your body.

There is another centre of energy at the crown of your head. Please focus your awareness in that centre. This is the crown centre. You may be able to feel or to sense the energy in that centre in some way, perhaps as tingling or coolness or some other sensation, or perhaps you won't — it doesn't matter, just be aware that it is there and focus your awareness in that part of your body.

There is a line of light that flows from the crown to the root, from the root to the crown. This line of light flows through the centre of your being. Allow your focus of awareness to flow down the line of light from the crown to the root and up from the root to the crown. You may be able to see or to sense the energy flowing along that line of light. If you are, fine; if you're not, just imagine it.

There is a centre of balance on the line of light. As you follow the flow of the energy from the root to the crown, the crown to the root, be aware of that centre of balance. Breathe into that centre of balance.

As you breathe into the centre of the line of light, be aware of the breath energising the centre and of the entire line becoming brighter and stronger.

Be aware of the line of light flowing from the centre of your being down through the root centre, down through your legs and feet, into the earth, and on down to the centre of the earth.

Feel the line of light connecting your centre with the heart of the earth.

Be aware of any confusion and tension and static within you, and allow it to drain down through this line of light into the earth. Be aware of the earth taking this energy, cleansing and purifying, transforming and strengthening it, and returning it to you as warm, powerful, loving, nurturing energy.

Allow yourself to become aware of that nurturing, warm energy of the earth lifting up through you, lifting and cradling every cell of your being. Be aware of the energy rising through your feet and through your entire being.

Breathe in again to the centre of the line of light, the centre of your being.

Follow the line of light from the centre of your being upward, up through your crown, to the centre of the universe. Be aware of it rising to the source of the creative life force.

Be aware of the energy at the centre of the universe, the vital force of life, the source of wisdom, of creation, of compassion. Allow yourself to feel that powerful, wise, creative, and loving energy radiating down the line of light into your being. Allow it to flow down through your crown, through the centre of your being, down through your root centre, and into the earth.

Be aware of the earth's energy rising through you like a warm fountain.

Be aware of the energy flowing down through you, like living light illuminating every particle of your being.

Be aware of the warm energy of the earth in the centre of your being. Be aware of the sparkling energy of the heavens in the centre of your being. Experience these energies combining and radiating through your entire being.

These two exercises, *Breathing in Truth* and *Line of Light* are both very simple in principle. They are also potentially very powerful. In order for them to work in stressful situations, we need to practise them in calm moments until we are very good at them.

Getting Help

Mental confusions are often easily resolved when we get some objective help. Sometimes all we really need is to talk a thing through and the solution becomes obvious. At other times, our confusion may be deeper or the situation much more complex, and we may need the help of a professional to sort it out. Financial advisors, lawyers, psychologists, and other specialists each have their own area of expertise in which they may offer us help. The more intractable the problem, the more we need good assistance.

We have looked, now, at some of the aspects of being mentally and physically earthed and centered, and it is time to consider the emotions. I have left them until last because I believe them to be the most important. In most cases our physical and mental imbalances have their roots in the emotions.

41. Adrift on a Stormy Sea

We have considered the physical and mental aspects of being centered and being grounded, but there is much more to it than that. Being physically and mentally earthed and centered *helps* us to be emotionally centered, but it doesn't *cause* it. In fact, much of the time, being out of balance emotionally is the root cause of mental or physical imbalance.

Emotions are the most difficult thing from which to detach ourselves. We can look with some objectivity at our physical bodies (though not necessarily at our emotional response to them) and we can also, especially with the help of others, examine our thoughts for things like rationality and logical consistency. However, our emotions just *are* — they are a-rational. They have an internal logic of their own, but it is based on unconscious assumptions that we may not consciously recognise.

Emotional stability is something that people sometimes think of as not-feeling, as a state of emotional blankness. That is not at all what stability is. A person who is emotionally stable is one who can feel great joy or deep sorrow, who can laugh and cry, who can empathise with others and yet be clear about their own feelings, who can experience pleasure and pain and know the difference — and who can do all these things when they are appropriate in the moment. Then they can let go of them and *come back to centre.*

When we are well balanced, we have emotional flexibility, yet never lose our ground in reality. This enables us to return to our normal state when the crisis or situation is over, and that normal state is a feeling of warm and vital aliveness. Children seem to do this a lot, going from tears to peace as soon as the source of pain or fear is removed. As we learn to measure our self-worth by external standards (money, possessions, the approval of others, parental expectations, et cetera) we seem to lose much of this sense of all-rightness in ourselves. We replace it with fear of the future, a prime cause of ungrounded emotions.

There are a number of things we may do which indicate that we are uncentered and ungrounded emotionally.

We deny what we feel. Either we don't approve or simply can't admit (perhaps because it would hurt too much) that we feel what we do feel. A sign of this is when others frequently ask why we are upset, and we answer that we aren't.

We 'project' our feelings onto others — we think that someone else is feeling what we are feeling. Very often this is accompanied by denial of what we do feel. This is very noticeable when other people do it.

We are away up one minute and utterly cast down the next, as if we were on an emotional roller-coaster.

Our feelings change quickly and frequently in response to the emotions of others around us.

We don't know what we feel.

We don't feel anything.

We are locked into one emotion, especially an extreme one. We experience extreme and persistent emotional states.

We believe that everyone is looking at and judging us. Sometimes this is associated with projection.

We believe that we can read other's feelings clearly at all times. We may even think we know more about their feelings than they do.

We feel responsible for the sorrows of the world.

We are constantly angry about the state of the world.

We 'sacrifice' our lives 'for the benefit of others'.

We seek peace at any price.

We have fears that those around us regard as irrational.

We are very rigid and judgmental about the behaviour of others and their expression of emotion.

We feel a need to manipulate or control others in order to feel secure. We may excuse this as being 'for their own good'.

We feel 'drained' by others when they express their emotions.

We feel worthless or unworthy of love and good things and success.

We look to others to supply our emotional needs and blame them for our unhappiness.

We usually try to give others what we think they want — often without being asked to do so.

We feel exhausted and 'drained' by crowds.

One of our emotions is in control of our behaviour and thoughts.

A long list, isn't it? Most of the symptoms of mental and physical ungroundedness could be on this one as well. Many of these imbalances could not occur if we were not suppressing or repressing many of our own feelings.

Suppression & Repression

There is a kind of blankness of walled off feelings which some people regard as 'self-control'. This is actually a very dangerous state. Suppressed and unresolved emotion has a part in the creation of many major diseases — and a lot of minor ones as well. Awareness of the psychosomatic factors in illness is finally beginning to receive the attention it deserves, and it is now more widely understood that our feelings can not only make us feel badly, they can actually make us seriously ill. This awareness is encouraging more of us to look for ways of handling emotion that don't involve either suppressing our feelings or battering everyone around us with them, sometimes to our own cost.

When we are centered and earthed emotionally, we resolve our emotions rather than repress them. We recognise what we are feeling when we are feeling it, and we respond appropriately. Sometimes it is good to express our feelings, while other times it is better for us to find safe ways of acknowledging and respecting them without 'going public'. When we are centered and earthed, we have a much better sense of the long-term effect and results of our own emotional response on ourselves and others. We can then more objectively decide just what we want to do.

There is an important difference between suppressing our emotions and recognising and accepting our feelings, yet not blindly reacting to them. When we suppress them, pretending they are not there, they remain with us, like dirt swept under the carpet, where they continue to contaminate our emotional state. If, on the other hand, we recognise our feelings, and accept that is how we really feel (even though we may not admire ourselves for it), we are then able to look for creative and constructive ways of releasing or expressing the emotion — ways that do not create even worse problems for ourselves and others. The really vital thing is that we do recognise our feelings and acknowledge them. What we then do with and about them is our choice.

42. Calming the Waters

Meditation helps wonderfully in calming the waters during or after an emotional storm, but there are other things we can do as well, including some specific meditation-like centering techniques. Taking these other helpful steps in calming and clearing ourselves, of course, means that we also get more out of meditating. We can create another positive feedback loop in ourselves.

Clearly, one of the first steps in sorting ourselves out, is to recognise what we really feel — all of it. Our feelings may be contradictory and this sort of thing is confusing. When we are confused, we tend to become ungrounded. We are perfectly capable of feeling several things *at the same time.* For example, we might feel anger, love, hurt, and compassion toward one person all at once. Sorting these feelings out and understanding and acknowledging the conflicts and confusions that exist within us are the first things we need to do in handling our emotions.

Our emotions basically come from two sources. One source is our present situation (often coloured by past experience), and the other source is past experience that we are still re-living, our habitual emotional responses to life. Changing an emotional habit is difficult. The habit of anger or fear, for example, is like a drug addiction. Both emotions cause us to release adrenalin into our bodies, and we can be 'hooked' on the feeling of excitement and 'aliveness' it gives us. It's very similar to being addicted to caffeine — except we don't even have to admit that we have an addiction. Addictions are habits with teeth — they dig in and don't want to let go. However, any habit can be changed if we want to badly enough. It just requires persistence and persistence and persistence.

Changing an emotional habit that keeps us ungrounded is like trying to get our balance on a rock, compared with dealing with our emotions in an ongoing situation. Where the external pressure is still active, we are like someone trying to get their balance of a surfboard on the crest of a large wave. It can be done, but it's tricky. One thing that helps a lot is to practise and practise and practise earthing and centering techniques until we are so good at them that we can use them even under great stress.

Obviously, if we have serious or long-standing problems, we would benefit from the support of a trained and experienced person, like a professional therapist or counsellor, as we work through our issues. Often even lesser problems are most constructively approached with some professional support. In addition to whatever help we receive from others, there are some very powerful meditative tools we can use to help ourselves become more centered and earthed emotionally. One of these is, again, working with our breath.

A Breath of Air

In several of the meditation techniques and in the earthing and centering exercises given earlier, you were asked to focus your attention upon your breath. There is an interesting physiological mechanism involving the breath. Abdominal breathing is relaxing — it is very difficult to maintain a state of anxiety when we are breathing down into the diaphragm. When we become excited or anxious, we tend to breathe into the upper chest, and this may become a habit if we are stressed over a period of time.

The interesting thing is that breathing in the upper chest alone is not only a result of anxiety — it also causes us to *feel* anxiety. Therefore, the habit of upper chest breathing causes us to feel a continual state of anxiety, and we then *look* for things to be anxious about. There is a Chinese proverb which says that the man who wants to beat a dog can always find a stick. And we can always find a hook to hang our worry on.

On the other hand, breathing into the lower abdomen tends to relax us, make us sleepy, and induce serenity. If you watch a baby sleeping, you will probably see that its ribcage hardly moves at all, but its abdomen moves quite strongly with its breath.

Breath that involves both chest and abdomen is helpful in inducing a state of relaxed alertness and is also helpful in our practice.

Right now is a good time to spend a few moments observing your own breath with one hand on your chest and the other on your abdomen. Just observe which hand moves the most, without making any changes. If you are not fully satisfied with what you experience, you can change it. Breathing patterns are habit, and all habits resist change, but we need not be their slaves. Like any habit, breathing patterns require only determination and persistence to change.

A gentle and non-forceful way of gradually changing a habit of anxious breathing is to do, at every opportunity, the following breathing technique.

Wave Breath

Sit like a mountain. Relax. Close your eyes.

Begin by simply observing your breath in your nostrils. Notice the inhalation and the exhalation, feeling the difference in temperature, pressure, moisture, and duration. Notice any difference between the left and right nostrils. Do not try to control the breath in any way — just observe it.

After five minutes or so of this (exact time is not important), imagine that you are inhaling through your navel, the breath rising up to the throat, and falling again to exhale through your navel. Imagine this with each breath, but do not make any effort to control the breath itself. Duration and depth may be quite variable, but do not make any effort to even them out. In fact you need pay no attention at all to these aspects of your breath.

Allow yourself to imagine your breath rising and falling in through the navel, up to the throat, down and out through the navel. Imagine your breath being like the waves on the shore, flowing in and up, down and out to sea — in the navel and up to the throat, down to the navel and out, as gently and peacefully as the waves rolling in, flowing out.

This exercise usually results in the breath *effortlessly* becoming deeper, smoother, and quieter. This gradual change takes place in its own time. It is not forced, but occurs in natural response to the image in our minds. Because the breath flows in both the abdomen and the chest, we are encouraged by our bodies to be in a state of relaxed alertness. The important thing in the exercise is to hold the attention upon the *imaginary* movement of the breath without making any conscious effort to change the depth or duration or movement of each breath.

There is another breath-centered exercise that is very grounding, but perhaps a little more difficult for many people. When the breathing exercise above has become easy for you, this is a more challenging one to move on to. It is grounding in the fullest sense and will probably take at least fifteen or twenty minutes, perhaps even longer, to do properly.

Earth's Breath

Imagine that you are inhaling through your feet. Imagine that the air you are inhaling rises out of the earth and the exhaling breath goes deeply back into the earth. The breath rises to your knees as you inhale, and then falls back through your feet as you exhale.

Once that becomes easy, let the breath rise through your feet to your hips, to the centre of your pelvis. When the breath has stabilized at that level, allow it it rise up to the level of your navel and solar plexus. Then up to your heart. Then your throat. Then the centre of your head. And finally up to the crown of your head.

Breathe from the earth, through your feet, up to the crown of your head for ten minutes or so, and then allow your focus to gradually change so that you are inhaling in the normal way and breathing deeply into the abdomen.

The next time you find yourself becoming anxious or upset in any situation, try doing one of the earthing breath exercises and see what effect it has on you and on the way you deal with the situation itself. If you have been habitually ungrounded, you may well find that this gives you an amazing sense of control and power simply because it breaks the anxiety habit of looking for something to worry about and expecting the worst. This allows you to use your own inner resources to the fullest.

43. Safe Travelling

One of the subjects that comes up again and again in working on earthing and centering is the issue of power. We are accustomed to thinking of a particular kind of power — the *power over* other things or other people. This is the power that people think they need in order to be safe and secure. The desire for power to control and manipulate other people is rooted in the beliefs that:

There is not enough for everyone.
I have to fight for what I want.
Other people are out to get me.
More for him means less for me.
I can't trust anyone.
I am weak and other people can push me around unless I attack first.
The world is a cruel and hostile place.
God is a Cosmic Gangster who created a Devil to tempt me into doing wrong so He can punish me for it and take everything away from me.

These beliefs and the many others like them are only beliefs — they are not true in any absolute sense, but we can make them true *for ourselves* by behaving as if they were real laws of nature. These are our projections and fantasies, and they can easily become self-fulfilling prophecies. And these fears and insecurities are the motivation behind the desire to have *power-over* other people.

The worst of having *power-over* is that we can never have enough. We extend the boundaries of our area of control and all this does is gives us a longer boundary to defend. And it makes us a more appealing target for others who think in the same way. The kind of thinking that says, 'if I just have thus-and-so, I can be happy' or 'if I could only have so much in the bank, I will be secure' is never satisfied, because it comes from an *inner insecurity* which can never be fully comforted or satisfied by the *power-over* things or people in the world. No matter how much we have, that inner voice continues to reiterate that it is scared, it's in danger, it's not safe. It is entirely a programmed emotional voice and is not confused by facts.

The really sad thing about these beliefs is that they cause people to expend all of their energy and time on the external world, never realising that it is the internal world that is amiss. And the internal world is seriously amiss. These ungrounded fears and insecurities not only cause us to seek *power-over* others, but they also cause us to erect defensive walls to protect ourselves.

We not only try to protect our personal selves, but we may also extend that protection to our possessions in quite irrational ways. I once knew someone who bought an expensive new carpet, covered it with plastic sheeting, and eventually wound up living in the kitchen while the new carpet rested virtually undisturbed in the rest of the house. Now, you may think this example is so extreme as to be ridiculous, but I once knew someone who did everything I described, and I have been in more than one house where the hostess rushed over with a little lacy thing to stick under my elbow, so that I wouldn't wear out the arm of the chair. And I knew a couple who bought a new car (which they did every two years). They got vinyl upholstery so the seats would be easy to clean — and covered it with expensive made-to-measure clear plastic seat covers so the vinyl wouldn't get dirty and they could still see the pretty upholstery — and then they put blankets over the plastic because it was too hot and miserable to sit on. People do these things, and other people shake their heads pityingly. But . . .

This it is only an external manifestation of something we *all* do inside ourselves.

When we are ungrounded and off-centre, we feel anxious. We know (somewhere inside ourselves) that, in that state of mind, we are not capable of using our intelligence clearly and our power fully. Because we feel anxious and insecure, we start to fuss over a fear and we take protective measures for it. Each 'protection' creates another 'vulnerability' — and on and on, forever escalating.

Some years back I was told by a teacher that I needed to give up all of my defences. I was quite taken aback by this and responded that, in this world, surely we actually *need* some defences.

She smiled and patted my knee and said, "No, dear. Only by giving up all of our defences can we become invulnerable."

Instantly, half of my mind said enthusiastically, 'Oh! Yes! Absolutely!' and the other half simultaneously held up a finger in alarm and said, 'Wait! This does not logically compute!'

After some discussion and an appeal for help, I agreed to try. Since then I have been working on discovering and letting go of my defences, which are disguised and hidden in so many tricky ways — some of them even pretend to be strengths. Over the years I have been finding that she was right. As I have learned to see what the defences were protecting, I see that I really don't need them at all. Each one that I find and release makes me lighter and stronger — stronger in a way that is flexible and resilient rather than rigid and breakable.

Meditation, in itself, helps us to be more earthed and centered. Being more earthed and centered helps us to practise meditation. And better practice helps us to be even more earthed and centered, around again and again in a lovely ascending spiral — which we can enhance by doing the grounding exercises as well. All through this we are becoming more clear-sighted, more balanced, more real in every aspect of life. We feel more stable and strong in ourselves, and when we feel stable and strong in ourselves we are power-full. Then, we don't need to play silly power games with ourselves and with other people and things.

We don't feel a need to prove our power by pushing other people around or by accumulating things. We don't need to protect ourselves from imaginary attack, because we see clearly, and we know when we are and when we are not really being attacked. We find our own strength, and we can say 'yes' when we want to, 'no' when we want to, and it's *our* choice, made for *our* reasons. When we are power-full, we can be gentle and kind; we don't need to be selfish, grabbing everything for ourselves. We feel secure. We know we can take care of ourselves; we can meet our own needs and still be able to offer generosity to others.

Most importantly, perhaps, if we are really earthed, we can see that we actually have more of some things when we freely give them away. For example, the more love we give, the more we feel love inside ourselves. If we can go so far with this as to love ourselves, we become love-full, and then we experience no shortage of that much valued energy. Feeling loved may give us a false sense of security (false, because someone else can take it away), but feeling love flowing through us gives us a sense of joy that no one else can take away — only we can decide to stop loving and stop experiencing the flow of love energy.

We don't need to try to 'make' others give love to us, we don't need to be frightened of losing love, and others can't blackmail us by threatening to withhold it from us. We don't want or need to play power games with something that passes for love. To do so would stop the flow of the energy in ourselves. We realise that we can simply give love unconditionally because we are love-full and overflowing, and this does not depend on anything outside ourselves. But to do any of this, we have to be centered in ourselves and earthed in reality, rather than in fear. The Plain of Reflections must reflect clarity and the Sea of Changes needs to be still. This clarity and quiet and openness is what creates the space in ourselves which fills with serenity, joy, peace.

You now have the basic practical information — and some not-so-basic information as well — that you need to meditate effectively. In the last two parts of this book, we are going briefly to consider the influence of meditation on psyche and spirit.

We need to remember that meditation is not just something we do in our heads; it is something we do with our whole selves — body, mind, emotions, and spirit — and it affects us on all those levels.

Part IX

On the Wings of Transformation

44. *The Dragon & the Serpent*

Abraham Lincoln said 'A house divided against itself cannot stand' — and he was right. Yet, most of us are divided against ourselves. Part of us says 'yes', part of us says 'no', and other parts take sides and contribute to the argument. The Plain of Reflections is fragmented into small kingdoms, isolated from one another by deep canyons, where dragons creep in the darkness, and there are bottomless chasms below the Sea of Changes, where sea serpents from the dawn of time still dwell.

When we consider our source of resistance to inner transformation and to the realisation of our potential, there is a special part of ourselves that we need to recognise. We have something very ancient and simple-minded in us. It may have something to do with the patterning in our brain stem, the 'old brain' or 'hind brain'. This is the most primitive part of our mental equipment, and it has to do with rote response, habit, reflex, and our need for routine and ritual, along with other things. Whether this resistance comes from that part of our brains or not, there is a part of ourselves which has ideas like 'I did this before and survived — if I continue do it I will continue to survive' and 'this is new and unfamiliar — if I do it I might not survive' and 'this hurts — never do it again' and 'this feels good — do it as often as possible'.

You see how the pattern works? It's the way a puppy or a baby or any primitive creature learns when their learning is based purely on the pleasure/pain response and simple survival. This part of ourselves, an ancient inner dragon, a cold and wingless crawler in the depths, is not capable of theorising things like, 'if this feels good, then that should feel even better' or 'this behaviour worked once, but it probably won't get me what I want in the future' or 'if I try this a new way, it might work better than the old'.

It does not speculate or look forward (the function of the forebrain); it only has hindsight. It doesn't have imagination and cannot conceive of any feeling or behaviour it has not previously experienced. When pushed to change, it calls on the serpent in the depths of the Sea of Changes. This call makes the serpent radiate fear, causing tumult in the sea and generating storms that sweep the plain.

We may think this dragon-thinking sounds stupid, but on the whole it seems to work fairly well. Reptiles have survived a long time this way, although they are certainly not the powers in the land they once were — and their decline has been attributed to their inability to change their behaviour and to invent and try new responses, as mammals can. And of course, earth-bound dragons and sea serpents are virtually extinct, except for the ones at the back of our brains. If we think about it, we can recognise the people we know who are exceptionally strongly influenced by this part of themselves. They cannot make changes easily, they natter on about the 'good old days' and 'what was good enough for my father is good enough for me', and they would much prefer all the world to remain unchanged. It doesn't, of course, and they find that difficult.

This kind of programmed-by-experience response is there in all of us. It is behind that first impulse to say 'no' to something new, just because it is new. In addition to this, we have certain deep level automatic responses, things we learned as infants and as very small children. They have to do with how we get other people to take care of us and to meet our needs. As small children we *must* have others care for us, because we cannot survive on our own. Because this is an early survival issue, it becomes linked into the ancient part of the brain with the automatic yes-no, pain-pleasure programming.

This is a much more important issue than is generally recognised. All of us learn in infancy (or perhaps are even born knowing) that survival depends on getting others to take care of us in every aspect of life. Our entire survival depends on being either so charming or so demanding that others fulfill all our needs. It is this that traps us into the illusion that our security depends on the love and approval — or at least the attention — of others and *will always continue to do so*.

If we let this dragon in the depths rule us, it means we can never grow up. We just continue to be dependent children. We cannot, for example, be self-employed — we need a boss to relate to and depend upon. If we are good, doing as we are told and pleasing him, he will take responsibility for us, seeing that we are told what to do, shown how to do it, and taken care of financially. The trend in many large companies today is toward increasingly parental behaviour, encouraging this dependency. We can be children forever. On the other hand, being self-employed does not mean we have become independent adults. We may have rich and supportive parents lurking in the background, or we may have developed strategies to compensate for our fears, without resolving them.

This same basic belief that we cannot become self-responsible adults means that many husbands and wives set up unspoken agreements wherein the wife depends upon the husband for money and keeping the car going and all that, while the husband depends upon the wife for necessary aspects of daily living, like child care, properly cooked food, clean clothes, and an orderly home. This kind of mutual dependency is especially powerful because neither person really feels safe without the other. This particular example is changing in our society, but not as much as some people may think — and not without a lot of stress in people who were brought up to think of security in one way and are now being asked to behave in a way that does not provide that illusion of security.

There are many other examples of this. We may need others to be kind to us because we are not kind to ourselves (and indeed, we may have learned to manipulate others into kindness by being unkind to ourselves). We may need people to protect us because we cannot say 'no' when we need or want to, and we may also resent it when someone puts us in a position where we really want to say 'no' — and don't. Saying 'no' might risk losing the approval or care of someone else. We may need people to love us because we haven't learned to love ourselves. If that is so, we can only understand love in terms of pay-offs and dominance-submission.

Now, I am *not* saying that it is 'wrong' to work for a paternalistic corporation or to be married or involved with other people. We can be independent adults and still be employed by someone, married to someone, and cooperate with others. Alternatively, we can be self-employed, single, or sailing around the world single-handed, and we may still not have really resolved our fears about being unsupported by others.

Becoming an independent adult is something that happens inside us or not at all. If we do grow up, we are free to choose what kind of life we want to lead rather than being directed by an unconscious programme buried within us. If we don't, we are robot-slaves to our own unconscious fears, the dragon and the serpent within. The serpent is power and energy, and when we express that as fear and direct it against ourselves, it is a painful and difficult experience.

The dragon in the depths assumes that nothing changes as we grow older — we do not become bigger, stronger, or wiser. This belief gets its power and conviction from the fact that, once upon a time, we really were helpless infants, dependent on others for the important and basic necessities of life. It would have us remain always the same. However, there is another force in us that urges us to grow. The dark dragon of the depths is counter-balanced by the bright dancing dragon of the sky, a freely-flying, translucent, golden being.

45. The Dragon that Soars

There is a bright dragon that inhabits the Plain of Reflections — or at least, the air above it. We seldom actually see it, but its wild and magical call, pitched above our normal hearing range, resonates throughout our beings. It calls us to learn to fly above the chasms and canyons, to transcend the dark, ancient dragons of insecurity and rote response. It sings to the serpent, deep in the sea, of transcendence and joy, and evokes its power for transformation.

We are invited to reach beyond the known to the unknown, to venture and explore new ways of being, to take risks, to be courageous.

We are invited to accept responsibility for ourselves, to recognise that we are in charge of our own thoughts and feelings and behaviour.

We are invited to recognise that, with the acceptance of responsibility, there comes an accompanying power — the power to choose and direct our own lives, the power to care for ourselves.

We are invited to understand that this power is the only real security there is in this world, a security that rests on what is within rather than on what we can coax or manipulate others into giving us.

We are invited to accept and even to love ourselves. If we cannot do that we can never accept real love from others. Without genuine self-love we can only accept counterfeit versions that rely on dependency and 'payments' for continuance.

We are invited to be kind to ourselves, to treat ourselves with generosity.

We are invited, simply, to become adults, to be no longer dependent upon others to meet our basic physical and emotional needs in subtle and not-so-subtle ways.

We are invited to establish relationships with others based on sharing from strength rather than on clinging from fear.

One of the things the practice of meditation does for us is to bring us into closer contact with the dancing dragon of the heights and the light. It gives us objectivity and detachment and helps us to see that the view of the dark dragon is not entirely true, but is only the very limited understanding of someone who lives at the bottom of a deep canyon.

46. Riding the Dragon

The question then arises, which part of ourselves do we choose to attend to? The dragon in the canyon or the one in the sky? The first offers (but doesn't always deliver) safety and security, while the other offers risks and adventure and the glamour of the unknown. This question revolves around what kind of commitment we have made to ourselves about our lives. Is it a commitment to holding on, to playing it safe, to staying small? Or is it a commitment to fulfil all of our potential for growth, to live as richly and fully as we can?

If our commitment is to life in a bomb shelter, meditation is not for us, because it leads us out into the light and into adventure. If the dark dragon rules, we fear that kind of life. When it is allowed to actually dictate our course, rather than to merely advise and caution, we are apt to spend our lives in a dark hole in the ground. On the other hand, if we do want growth and adventure, we must remember that the dragon in the depths is not our enemy. We need it. It can be the one who cautions us from flying off blindly, without reasonable preparation and forethought, into the unknown.

Alternatively, if our commitment is to a life of growth and to the realisation of our creative potential, we mustn't let the fiery dragon of the sky run away with us. We need to avoid the simplistic trap of thinking that all risks are good just because they are risky and because they show our willingness to adventure. We need to find a balance between the urgings of the two dragons.

It is not up to me or anyone else to tell you what you should do with your life. It belongs to you to spend as you wish. What I am trying to do myself is to grow my own wings. Then I can listen to both dragons and choose my own way, balanced between realistic caution and expansion into creative potential. And I can fly the moonlit path across the Plain of Reflections, across the Sea of Changes, and up the mountain to the Place of Light.

47. Growing Our Own Wings

Let's try a small exercise.

Imagine that the one you most love or ever have loved is in front of you at this moment, and allow yourself to really feel all the love and tenderness you have for that person.

Once you have established that feeling of love in yourself, release the other person from your awareness, and direct all that love toward yourself, just as you are right now — virtues and faults, assets and drawbacks, hopes and fears, 'good' and 'bad'. Make no judgements; don't even think about any of these things.

Simply love yourself with all your heart.

No other being is involved in this love, either in giving or in receiving.

Continue doing this for ten minutes, allowing the quality and intensity of the love to continually increase.

How did that feel? Could you do it without encountering any resistance in yourself, any temptation to slide off into thinking about something else? What sort of other feelings or ideas came to your mind? What do they tell you about how you really feel about yourself?

All right. The instinctive, inborn baby within us needs security. It is programmed (probably genetically) to try to evoke love from others because, if they love it, they will take care of it. If we don't love it (ourselves), we don't take proper care of it (ourselves). It panics and takes control of our lives, frantically trying for the love, approval, and care of others. It never discovers that we (the adult part of us) can satisfy its needs for love and security.

We need to convince this inner infant that we are mature, responsible, loving adults who can be trusted to take care of it.

If we act from the adult part of our personality and convince the inner baby that it is cared for and secure, it will do what satisfied babies do and either gurgle happily to itself or go to sleep. It will certainly not lie awake urging us to play dominance/submission games or manipulating others into caring for us or howling with jealousy.

Suppose you truly loved yourself — how would you treat yourself? Would it differ from the way you treat yourself now? Would you be less critical? Less demanding? Less angry with yourself? More compassionate? More caring? More generous? More self-disciplined? Kinder? More careful of yourself and your energy? Would you change the way you feed yourself? The way you dress? The kind of work you do? Would you continue to let other people treat you the way they do now?

Can this baby within trust you to look after it lovingly and well?

Meditation can have an important role in helping us to learn to love ourselves. Apart from the obvious fact that meditation is a way in which we can take better care of ourselves and enhance the quality of our lives, it also helps us to discover an aspect of our being with which we may be unacquainted. This part of ourselves is supremely loving and lovable —

so much so that many people who come into contact with it think that it must be something outside of themselves. We do not easily believe that we could possibly have something so wonderful within us.

In fact, we are usually so convinced of our own essential undesirability that we feel that it is wrong or selfish to love ourselves. Yet, the only way we can truly love others is from a position of being love-full. When we are 'in love' with another, we tend to be more loving all around. Imagine then how loving we would be to the world at large if we cared for ourselves so much that we felt completely secure in that love. This is not selfishness, it is sheer common sense: to love ourselves increases our capacity to love others.

Until we develop the unconditional love, we can use our not-love for ourselves to help us grow into loving, just as we embraced the enemy in overcoming resistance to meditation and used it to help find and close the cracks in our consciousness through which it entered. For example, jealousy is considered a 'negative emotion', and when we have it, we don't like to admit to it. We usually prefer to blame others for hurting us, rather than acknowledging that we are being dependent and demanding. Suppose that, instead of trying to suppress or ignore it, we actively use it to help us grow?

What if, when we feel jealous about something, we acknowledge the feeling to ourselves and try to discover exactly what unfulfilled need it is speaking to us about? It usually has to do with insecurity — insecurity about love or attention or being cared for. How carefully and completely can we define that unfulfilled need?

We may be jealous of someone because they have something we think we want, but it isn't really the object that we want — it is the feeling of self-esteem or fulfilment we believe having that object would give us. What is that feeling we want?

If we are jealous of another's love or attention, what is it we really want from that love or attention? How would it make us feel better about ourselves? Do we need to feel more valued? More secure?

And then, what can we do *ourselves* to give *ourselves* these feelings? How can we best show the love or caring we need to our own being?

In trying to do this, we may learn things about ourselves that we don't like. We may have denied or projected them onto others in the past, but now we are being honest with ourselves and recognising our own shadows, the shadows which darken our inner world, casting a pall of gloom over the Plain of Reflections and darkening and polluting the Sea of Changes. By recognising and transforming that energy from destructive to constructive, we are releasing the life force that has been bound in darkness, in the fearful chasms of the deep sea, and we are giving ourselves new life. When we do this, jealousy turns around and becomes a positive force in our lives — the dragon in the depths is lifted up into the light and can see what it really needs in order to feel secure. And instead of waiting and hoping that what we need will fall into our canyons in front of our noses, or that someone else or the fates will give it to us, we can just give it to ourselves.

It takes a lot of attentive listening and clarity to get this one right, but we have been learning that kind of listening and clarity in our meditation practice, haven't we? And meditation helps us in learning to love ourselves in other ways as well.

When we meditate with an intense, yet relaxed, concentrated focus, we can invite all the disparate parts of ourselves into the meditation process. Most of the time we are like a badly organised committee that cannot even agree on what it wants to do. Each individual on our Plain of Reflections has its own desires and needs. Some are ruled by the dragon and sea serpent in the depths, others by the flying, dancing dragon, still others by their own confusion. A few may even be clear-sighted and ruled by good sense. How do you suppose it would affect us if, just for a moment, all those voices became one — and that one rang as clear as a bell?

Imagine the change in energy if you were in a room with many people, all babbling away about their own concerns, and gradually everyone began to hum the same note, until they were all singing one bright, plangent tone.

Think of the difference between ordinary light, with its waves scattering in different directions, and the coherent light of a laser beam, with all of its waves moving in unison. It is the laser beam that has cutting power and the greatest brilliance.

When we manage to gather all of our fragmented selves together in meditation, bringing ourselves into a single focus of mind and heart and energy, we shift into a completely different way of being. In this, the mystical experience, there is no longer a self that observes and a self that experiences. There is only Self. The experiencing of this Self has a profound effect on our psyche.

Psychotherapy starts at the top, in consciousness, and gradually works down, but the transformational energy of fully focused meditation radiates through our whole being simultaneously, cutting through the darkness and confusion like a beam of clear and coherent light. When this happens, it usually takes us months, perhaps even years, to consolidate and integrate the change in our consciousness.

Every time we meditate, we allow that beam of light to shine through us. Sometimes it may be weak, with many of the rays still scattered, and sometimes it may be strong, but it always has some effect. The more of ourselves we can bring into the meditation process, the stronger the light is. It takes a great deal of light, much meditation practice, to cut through the confusion in our psyches. On the occasions when we do reach that total focus, when the radiance shifts from partial into complete, it lights up our entire being. Not for nothing is this experience called 'illumination'.

Even when we manage to get it all together, the light usually only shines for a moment before we lose it again. This is just as well because we need time to integrate the changes that arise from this experience. Otherwise, we'd be so dazzled by all the light that we'd be unable to see our way. We need this light in doses that our psyche can manage and integrate. We need the day to day experience of a little more and a little more just as much as we need the occasional wild power of the pure and perfectly attuned light. And our wings — well, our wings are made of light.

There is a deep
dark note,
the slow breath of a timeless god,
played on a *bansuri* flute.
This song
wants to play me,
but every time
I am almost attuned,
it shakes me apart.
No rigid places, no bones

in my spirit, no shadow
can live
in that sound. I need to be
pliant and hollow, a green reed
in the wind,
so that slow descant
can breathe through.

This, of course, brings up the question of where we cross the line between psyche and spirit. Is there such a line, or are psyche and spirit simply aspects of the whole? If the psyche is the Plain of Reflections and the Sea of Changes and if the spirit is the mountain in the centre, how can we suppose they are separate? They are all rooted in the same earth, and we move naturally from one to the other.

Part X

On Ascending the Mountain

48. Which Way Is Up?

In climbing the mountain at the centre of being to reach the Place of Light, the peak of our potential, we find that there are many paths. Some paths lead part way up and stop at a little camping place on a plateau, where people may pretend, if they like, that they have reached the top. Some ways join with other paths as they climb, some seek the gentlest way (but are still a fairly stiff climb), and some boldly run straight for the top, ascending steep cliffs and traversing deep crevices.

Many religions offers us a path to the Place of Light, but not every religion is appropriate for every spiritual traveller. In fact, some people seem to need to cut their own path, or perhaps they follow a hidden trail that hasn't been used much for centuries.

In order to make the rest of our discussion easier, let us define the terms 'religious' and 'religion' in a narrow way as pertaining to formal systems of belief, usually stemming from a scripture or from the specific teachings of an inspired individual. And let us define 'spiritual' in a much broader way, which not only includes the various religions, but also includes the sense we all have of something Other and of the importance of abstract principles in daily life. In some people this sense may be vague and unfocused, in a few it may be quite suppressed, and in some it may be a clear and active force in their lives, within or without the framework of a formal religion.

Meditation techniques have long been a central part of most religions, even though the majority of believers in any given faith may not practise meditation themselves — indeed, they may even view it with deep suspicion. The reason for this widespread lack of understanding about these techniques is that most religions have two main branches: the *exoteric* and the *esoteric*.

Exoteric religions focus on the idea that there *has been* a divine revelation, that Jesus or the prophets or Mohammed or Buddha or Lao T'su or whoever has spoken and that is The Word. This word is simply to be understood, interpreted by the authorities of the church where necessary (this is where divisions and sects develop), and obeyed by the faithful. Exoteric religions have to do with behaviour and 'doing' and faith. The exoteric followers of any religion are usually in the majority.

On the other hand, the esoteric side of a religion focuses on inner spiritual growth and on 'being' and experience. This is 'the path of the mystic' and it is practised by many Cistercians, Benedictines, Quakers, and others within the Christian Church, as well as by Zen Buddhists, Sufis, and others who follow the mystical path within the various religions of humankind.

Many religions start as esoteric, with a core of belief and simple ritual to focus the spiritual intention and self-discipline of the mystic. However, the belief system and ritual, in themselves, may then attract other followers who are not presently suited, whether emotionally or mentally, to tread the long and difficult path of inner growth and the way of silence. These new followers give their attention to the exoteric outer path of dogma and ritual and rules, elaborating upon them as questions of interpretation arise. They may ignore or discourage the development of the inner spiritual life. Nearly every religion seems to develop this schism within itself.

As a result of this split, many people who consider themselves Christian, for example, have little knowledge of esoteric Christianity, even though it was an important part of the early Christian church. I think this is a very great pity, and it is probably one of the principle reasons why Christianity has become, to so many people, either a nominal religion without real meaning in their lives, or else an outmoded dogmatic and ritualistic irrelevancy to modern life.

Please do not misunderstand me here — I am not saying the exoteric path is invalid, or that everyone should follow the esoteric path of their religion. Many people are not temperamentally suited to the path of the mystic, and each of us needs to find our own way up the mountain in our own time. However, for those who are so suited (and they are our consideration here), a religion that does not include some form of meditation may seem quite barren and sterile. The esoteric path is the path of experience rather than of faith, and meditation evokes the particular kind of experience that is sought — the mystical experience.

The exoteric branch of a religion may be divided into many sects, each sincerely believing the others to be wrong in some important way. This is much less likely to be true of the esoteric members of the faith. In fact, they may often draw upon other religions for techniques and disciplines to help them along their path. For example, I remember meeting a Franciscan priest, devout in his religion, who just had spent two years studying Zazen with a Zen master. This kind of breadth of vision and interest in other disciplines is not unusual among mystics. People for whom religion is an external (exoteric) structure may not understand the view of the person to whom it is an internal (esoteric) experience, and this misunderstanding can work both ways. Those of us to whom the path of the mystic seems the only conceivable path may assume that the external focus of exoteric religion is only a superstructure for the mystical experience. It may come as a real surprise to a 'natural' mystic that this is not so.

I well remember the amusement of one of my teachers, a Jesuit-trained former priest, when I first discovered that there were people who believed in God and who held religious beliefs and principles purely because they had *authority* for this in the Bible and in the writings of the church fathers. I was really amazed by this. He laughed and remarked that there was something that would surprise me even more — that some people believed in God because they felt the existence of God had been proven by the use of rigorous logic. I was astonished — it had never occurred to me that anyone could or would believe in a higher power without the direct experience of mystical union.

The meditative techniques described in this book are not singular to any particular religion, and they can be practised by almost anyone without harming or denying their religious life in any way. In fact, they will enrich it. Many of the exercises are used by the esoteric branches of most religions for spiritual development. The same techniques for stilling the mind and relaxing the body are encountered in Hindu, Buddhist, Muslim, Jewish, Christian, and other sources.

The truth is, regardless of our religion, we all have the same physiological structure — and the same relaxation techniques work for all of us. We also have the same brain structure and fundamental mental processes, so that techniques for stilling the mind are cross-cultural. The meditation techniques we have discussed are just a few of the steps used on the many different religious paths to the Place of Light. None of them is unique to any one religion, nor are they inapplicable in other religious settings. Although there are many paths up the same mountain, the paths meet and cross in many places and all join together at the peak. And of course, the mystical experience is a 'peak experience'.

49. When the Going Gets Hard

Mountains are notoriously difficult to climb, and the spiritual mountain at the centre of the self is no less so than the material mountains of our world. In the practice of meditation, we occasionally reach a time when our meditation seems difficult and fruitless. These are often described as 'spiritual dryness'.

Dry Spells

Sometime we reach a point where we can't seem to focus on our technique, our ability to concentrate seems to desert us, and what meditation we do, if we do any at all, seems to do no good. We don't feel relaxed or restored; we just feel frustrated and futile. When we are about to break through an old habit or pattern within ourselves, we find it difficult to do anything but struggle with our resistance — and the more we struggle, the harder it seems to get.

At this point we usually have little fantasies, like: I just need to stop trying for a while and come back to it later when life is simpler. Yes and no. We do need to stop *trying* and just do the exercises, without running in circles after our resistance. We do *not* need to stop meditating — in fact, we desperately need to continue. We are close to something good, and if we stop now, it will bury itself again. Then later, when things are 'easier', we start again and continue until we reach the same point — where we stop again. We can go on repeating this cycle forever if we want to, but it seems only sensible to get through whatever it is and come out the other side.

In the worst stages of 'spiritual dryness' (I can easily think of stronger terms for it!) we may become quite depressed, feeling not only that what we are doing at the moment is futile, but also that what we have done in the past was also useless. We may even feel that we have been fooling ourselves in the past by thinking that we were making any sort of progress with meditation — or even that there is any sort of progress to be made by meditating or by doing anything else. Life looks very black. We *know* that we are hopeless, that our lives are without purpose and without meaning, and that we are no more than a disgusting blot on a pointless and illusory landscape.

None of it is true.

This is a time to seek help. If you belong to a formal religion, this is when you need your priest, minister, guru, or whatever. If your own doesn't seem to understand, find one who does. I fell into a fairly deep spiritual pit while in London one time. After a couple of grim and depressing weeks trying to sort it out by myself, I walked into Westminster Abbey (although I am not an Anglican) and asked for a priest. The man who came to talk to me had been through the same thing himself, had some very sound advice for me, and best of all, comforted me and showed me that this was a stage of growth rather than a failure. From being lower than the lowest worm (really, there is nothing wrong with worms), I went to being a person who had made a particular kind of mistake, had recognised it, had a sincere desire to do better, and now had some idea of where to start. I was so grateful.

This was a relatively easy problem with which to deal, and I already had a lot of tools for helping myself once I got pointed in the right direction. Some problems are more intractable and need more help than one discussion. Some may revolve around psychological problems and need a therapist to help, but you want to be careful with this. By no means all therapists are qualified (nor are all priests) to deal with the kind of problems we encounter while climbing the spiritual mountain. Basically, I suppose, they need to have been there themselves. It really does need to be more than just something they learned from a book or from observing other people's experience.

The rule is, if you don't find the right person on the first try, keep on trying.

In the meantime, while you are looking for help, there are some things you can do for yourself.

1. Keep on meditating. If you are not working with 'expectant gratitude' try it. It will probably be very difficult. You might start by just focusing on a warm spot in the area of your heart.

2. Try to arrange to have someone else meditate with you. If you can meditate with a group regularly, do so.

3. Cosset yourself. Get gentle massages. Eat soothing and healthy food. Be kind and generous to your body.

4. Do lots of earthing exercises, especially Breathing In Truth.

5. Spend time with gentle and kind people, doing gentle and interesting things.

6. Do something of service to others every day. Perhaps do some kind of volunteer work, if you have time.

7. Keep gently occupied in positive activities. Strictly avoid activities and people who make you feel worse about yourself.

8. Don't discuss the problem with a lot of people. Sympathy will not make it better, but it may well make it worse, and talking about your misery will just reinforce it. Find one or two people who understand something about what is happening and discuss it only with them.

After the experience of such spiritual dryness, we usually burst forth into insight. It can be almost as difficult to stay balanced and earthed in this sudden realisation as it was in the depressed state we have just been through. We have reached a peak on the mountain, possibly even the summit, and we tend to be so stunned and amazed by this that we immediately fall back down.

Integrating Insight

Insight produces a change of consciousness, perhaps a radical one, which necessarily includes a new way of seeing the world and ourselves. This new way of seeing may be a marvelous insight or change within ourselves that abruptly allows us to fulfil much more of our potential as magical beings. Or perhaps we have an instant cataclysmic flash of insight about ourselves, and it really shakes us, stirs us, upsets us. It throws light into one of the dark, hidden places in our own being, and we say, 'Oh, God, I've been doing this awful thing and its been hurting me and poisoning my life and my relationships with others and hurting them. Please, I don't ever, ever want to do it again!'

Right.

And this 'awful thing' stems from a core belief, from one of the foundations of our world, a part of the dragon in the depths, something that is so deeply a part of us that until now we just accepted it as truth, as a condition of the world-as-it-is. But it isn't, and now we know that — we know it not only in our heads (which may have been suspecting it for some time), but also in our guts, in our deepest feelings, in our emotional bedrock. And we feel absolutely shattered. Or, if the realisation was one of joy, we feel incredibly high, completely out of this world, ecstatic beyond words, completely out of our minds.

Now what?

Well, the first thing is to remember to breathe, to earth and centre ourselves. The second thing is to say 'thank you' to whoever and whatever helped us to get here, including our own selves. Breathe. Ground. Centre. The third thing is to be gentle and loving with ourselves — we've just done some real growing and we deserve the best we can do for ourselves. Breathe. Earth. Centre. The fourth thing is to give ourselves time to thoroughly integrate this insight internally before we begin making radical changes externally — no rushing off to make atonement or to join a monastery or the Peace Corps or to save the world. Breathe. Earth. Centre. The fifth thing is to do as much physical work as we reasonably can — clean the house, do all those things the garden needs but rarely gets, go for long walks, play enthusiastically. Breathe. Earth. Centre. The sixth thing is to take responsibility for ourselves — we not only look after ourselves, but if we need help, we go get it. We don't wait for it to come to us. Breathe. Ground. Centre. And the last thing is, keep meditating.

It may seem as if I am taking all this too seriously, but I know from the experience of myself and many others that if we do meditation, as we have discussed it, with any perseverance and consistency, we will experience radical spiritual growth. And that growth will rock us back on our heels so hard we need to be very well balanced to keep from falling over backwards.

There is another thing that can really help us. We must recognise the divinity in others. Without that we are limited and isolated, left alone to cope with all of our problems. Yes, other people may not understand what is happening to us, they may have silly ideas about how to help us. But ... There is something within each of them that *does* know, and sometimes, perhaps often if you are lucky in your friends, that something within will speak. So listen. Don't talk, just listen.

And of course, the most helpful thing of all is to trust — trust that a loving universe is providing what we need even if we don't always like it much.

50. Finding the Place of Light

Everyone has their theories about what the mystical experience is and how it happens. My own is that, through meditation sometimes and through 'grace' at others, we come completely into focus. Normally we are like a discordant chord, a crash of dissonant sounds. In meditation, we keep bringing ourselves together, bringing in the straying and confused and opposing parts of ourselves, until we have but one mind and one heart. We each have within us many people — many different responses to any situation, contradictory impulses, different programmes created by various influences in our past. Each of these responses, impulses, and programmes within is like a person singing its own note, some in harmony and some in discord. In meditation, we bring those notes closer and closer, until finally there is only one sweet, plangent bell ringing out through time and space.

Our whole being is not merely harmonised by this, but made one. There is no longer any dichotomy between observer and observed. There is only one. We can describe nearly everything that happens to us because there is this split between the observer-self and the experiencing-self, but we cannot describe the mystical experience because we have dissolved and clarified into oneness in the *acetum fontis*, the universal solvent of the alchemists.

When this happens, we seem to shift gears, to transcend ordinary consciousness by orders of magnitude. What has just become one goes on to become One, and we connect with our true nature. We learn things from this union. In particular, there is one basic principle:

All that is is One, and that One is God.

Call it God or Allah or Buddha or the universe or any other name, the message is the same. We are unified with, part of, wholly within, and yet, paradoxically, the whole of a divine Oneness that spans the cosmos and reaches beyond into known and unknown, past, present, and future, time and space, matter and energy, all that is, was, will be, or could be, infinite and eternal. It Is, I Am, We Are — these all say the same thing.

All that is is One and that One Is.

Through meditation we discover something within us that is far greater than any idea we might possibly have of ourselves. We are far bigger on the 'inside' than on the 'outside' — and the 'outside world' is a part of us, too. This Self that we find is not our thoughts, it is not our bodies, it is not our feelings, it is not our visions, it is not our imagination, it is not any of the things we normally think of when we try to describe ourselves.

In fact, this Self is indescribable, although people have tried through the ages to describe it through poetry and prose, painting, sculpture, and virtually every form of art that has ever been invented. Everything, from stone circles to dance to mathematics, has been used to try to delineate this essential union — and everything falls short.

That prolific writer Anonymous wrote, 'The lifting of a finger disturbs the farthest star', and John Donne wrote, 'Send not to know for whom the bell tolls. It tolls for thee.' They and many others *know by experience* this one unalterable fact that we learn through, and only through, the mystical experience.

All that is is One, and that One is God.

Since this is a practical book on the practice of meditation, I should like to finish up with one last series of exercises. If you put your whole self, body and mind, heart and soul, into it, it will bring you to the mystical union, not just once but again and again.

Of course, **so will any other meditation technique you use**, if you approach it with the same single-mindedness.

It is important to remember that the mystical experience may not wait for you to be ready to do any specific technique — it comes when it will. Like lightning, it strikes where there is least resistance and greatest conductivity. When we are ready, it happens, no matter what technique we use.

Having said all that, this is still my favourite meditation path.

51. Thankfully Sitting

This is a Zazen technique, which I mentioned briefly before, called *shikan-taza*. *Shikan* means 'just' or 'nothing but'; *ta* means 'to hit'; *za* means 'to sit'. *Shikan-taza*, then, means 'just to sit intensely'. This technique is based on the understanding that all of us are, at core, enlightened beings. Enlightenment is our essential nature, but we have lost sight of that, and we believe ourselves to be separate, alone, confused, and many other things that are incompatible with the direct and immediate and continuing experience of enlightenment. All silent, one-pointed meditation is an exercise to bring us back to full awareness of our true nature, but this one especially focuses on that awareness.

Shikan-taza itself is an advanced meditation, requiring extensive preparation, and is not suitable for beginners — they probably would only become hopelessly frustrated. However, there is a given path to work through until we come to 'just sitting'. It may take months or years of practising of the first exercises before you are ready for *shikan-taza* proper, depending on your present ability to concentrate.

Remember, though, that there is no point in hurrying. There is nothing to be gained by doing so, and much to be lost. You might have a mystical experience the first day of the first stage, you might not have one for ten years. You are more apt to have that experience if you are working at the level that is right for you than if you are feeling stress and frustration caused by working with a technique that is not right for you at this time.

Preparatory Techniques

Level One
Center and earth yourself.

Sit like a mountain with your body well aligned.

With your eyes open, let your gaze rest on the floor or a blank wall in front of you.

Focus your awareness in your hara, *a place just a couple of inches in front of your spine and just below the level of your navel. Feel your breath there.*

Open your heart to feel a sense of expectant gratitude.

Count your breaths — one-inhale, two-exhale, three-inhale, four-exhale — up to the count of ten. Count the breath to ten again and again, until the meditation time is up.

Keep your mind alert, don't allow yourself to become dozy.

You may find it hard to hold all this together — expectant gratitude, focus in the *hara*, and counting the breath. In fact, at the beginning, you may feel that you can't even get it together to start. Just keep going through the steps. Sooner or later something clicks into place, and it all comes together — at least for a few moments. It needs to become a *gestalt,* a wholeness, a single experience, with each element inextricably combined in the whole.

When you realise that you have lost one or another element of the technique, simply go through all the steps again. Real patience is required here. However, even the times when it doesn't come together seem to do something lovely for us — unless we are so involved with our frustration that we don't let ourselves notice the benefits.

When you can do the exercise above for fifteen minutes without losing
count and holding the whole thing together, change to Level Two.

Level Two
*This is exactly the same as Level One, except for the way the breath is counted.
Count your breaths only on the exhalation. Count your breath to ten again and
again, until the meditation time is up.*

Keep your mind alert, fully attentive to each breath, be centered in the hara,
and focused in expectant gratitude.

Again, when you can do the above for fifteen minutes without losing
count and keeping the whole thing together, change to Level Three.

Level Three
*This is again exactly the same as Level One, except for the way the breath is
counted. Count your breaths only on the inhalation. Count the breaths to ten
again and again, until the meditation time is up.*

Keep your mind alert, focused on breath, hara, *and expectant gratitude.*

Once again, when you can do the above exercise for fifteen minutes
without losing count and keeping the whole thing going, change to
Level Four.

Level Four
*Once again, only the breath is changed. Be aware of your breath, be aware of
each inhalation and exhalation, but* do not count them — *just follow the
breath, in and out, being clearly aware of it.*

Keep your mind fully alert and aware.

When you can do the above exercise for fifteen minutes without losing
breath awareness, holding the feeling of expectant gratitude, keeping a
focus of awareness in the *hara*, and keeping your mind really alert, you
may be ready to try *shikan-taza* itself. If you try it, and find it too hard
for you at this time, just go back to Level Four until you feel you are
ready to come to it again. We do not gain points for trying to do any
stage before we are ready — we only get frustrated.

Just Sitting

Center and earth yourself.

Sit like a mountain, with your eyes open.

Focus your attention in your hara. Open your heart to feel a sense of expectant gratitude.

Hold your mind like a cloud — still and without boundaries, yet fully alert and aware; intensely concentrated, but without strain.

Let all these aspects become an integrated whole.

Be entirely involved with this, always bring back any part of yourself that wanders away, back to the hara, the expectant gratitude, the mind like a luminous cloud, all integrated into one.

If we do this, or any other meditation technique, long enough and diligently enough, we will have a mystical experience. We may have it while we are meditating, we may have it while washing the dishes or looking at a flower or riding the bus or standing in the rain or seeing the sunrise or listening to someone speaking. It happens when we are ready.

And when you have the mystical experience, then what? Is that it then? No, of course not. It is just another step along the way. This experience does something to us, shifts something in the bedrock of our personality. It takes time for all the effects of that experience to bubble up through the layers of our consciousness, changing them as it comes. And it takes more than one mystical experience to produce a *fully* enlightened human being. It is a lifetime process. There is no place for the journey to end.

52. Living in the Place of Light

Several years ago I asked a friend, who had been working seriously for a number of years on her spiritual development, how she would define a fully enlightened person. She gave me a very articulate description of such a person's characteristics. I asked her again while I was writing this book.

"I don't know," she answered in a slightly strained tone.

I reminded her that she had once given me a concise definition.

"Yes," she said, "I used to think I knew, but the longer I work at this the less I seem to know about that."

I don't know either.

Is it, like a Zen Buddhist said, a person who never reacts from old programming, but who sees the moment clearly and chooses the appropriate course? Is it the hermit in the desert, scourging himself and praying and avoiding sin? Is it the luminous, radiant nun in the Benedictine choir? Is it the person who always thinks of others first and does his best to be of service? Is it the yogi who can be cut and not bleed, control his heart rate at will, and drastically cut down his oxygen consumption without ill effects? Do any of these things have anything to do with enlightenment itself, or are they just steps on the paths? Perhaps some of them are even dead ends, leading only to dangerous precipices.

Are we like fish looking up through the surface and seeing a bird fly, trying to explain it in terms we can understand? When we get there, will we even recognise it ourselves?

One thing I suspect is that having had the mystical experience is not the criterion by which we can measure true enlightenment. I know too many people, myself included, who have had such experiences and still obviously have a lot of work to do on themselves. Some people have one such experience and seem to think that's it — and they stop right there, camping on the mountain and refusing to notice the heights they have not yet scaled. I do know that reaching the Place of Light, however briefly, leaves its mark on people — but so does climbing the mountain, even part of the way.

I used to think that an enlightened person was one who lived with the fierce, blazing light of mystical union as the bedrock of consciousness all the time and who had no shadows within himself to block it out, but now — well, I just don't know. But if I keep working at it, I'll eventually find out.

I am nothing —
no thing, no time, no space.
I am the empty wind
that blows across the Void.
Yet I am not
the wind, nor am I
the void.

I am the leaves
that fall
and become dust — the dust
that blows through space,
is immolated in the fires
of distant suns, and goes forth
again as light. And yet I am not
these things.

I am the phoenix, risen
from my own ashes,
still burning, my own light
too bright for me to bear. I am
all things and no thing.
I am one. I am none.
I am not-I. Only
the One Is.

Appendix A

Meditation Techniques

1. Sit. Relax. Think of a simple design such as a circle around a cross or some other easily visualised symbol. Visualise this during your entire practice period, but do not try to think about what it symbolises in any way.

The design should be kept simple. It should not be complicated, unbalanced, or scattered. Preferably it should be within a circular form and should have a well-defined centre. Use the same design each time.

2. Sit. Relax. Rest your hand in front of you so that you can look down at your thumbnail with your eyelids lowered. Look intently at your thumbnail, but without straining your eyes. Keep your eyes and eyelids relaxed.

Be aware of the movement of your breath in your abdomen. During the entire exercise, stay aware of your breath, and keep observing your thumbnail. Do not think about your thumbnail or try to be profound about it — just look at it attentively, as if it were the most interesting thing you have ever seen.

3. Sit. Relax. Count your breaths (each inhale and exhale as one breath) up to ten and then begin at 'one' and count them again up to ten. Repeat again and again through the practice time. When you lose count, start again.

Do not try to control your breathing in any way.

4. Sit. Relax. Tell yourself that you are now going to relax mentally and let your mind drift, not thinking about anything in particular. Allow

thoughts to form and to fade again without thinking about them in an analytical way or trying to control them. Let them be like bubbles rising up from the depths, and let them drift away again. You are just observing them come and go.

When the practice time is up, you can review these thoughts, if you wish, and see if any of them suggest insights into your attitudes and or behaviour patterns, but do not think about that while you are practising.

5. Sit. Relax. Choose a colour such as green, blue, lavender, or blue-violet. Think of a sphere of this colour and visualise it during your practice period.

Do not choose an active, energetic colour such as red, yellow, or orange.

Different colours, like different sounds, have varied effects on your system. Use your intuition to choose the right colour for yourself.

6. Sit. Relax. Become aware of your breath. Notice the inhalation, notice the exhalation. Now begin noticing the shift where the breath changes from inhalation to exhalation, from exhalation to inhalation. Be attentive to those shifts. Do not extend them or try to emphasise or control them in any way — just be aware of them. Count these shifts up to ten, then begin your count again. Repeat this throughout the meditation period.

Alternative: To make this exercise more of a challenge, don't count. Just note the shifts of the breath and keep your mind wholly focused on that.

The first version is suitable for beginners, the second for those with more experience.

7. Sit. Relax. Choose a two or three syllable sound which has no meaning to you but which is a pleasant sound. Use the same sound each time. Repeat the sound over and over, aloud or silently, or alternating between silently and aloud.

If you are doing it aloud, let the sound rise up from your lower abdomen.

Different sounds affect us in a variety of complex ways. Use your intuition to help you select the sounds that will be most helpful in creating harmony in your system.

8. Sit. Relax. Be aware of your breath. Observe the sensation of inhalation and exhalation. See how continuously and how closely you can observe and sense your own breath. Be aware of the movement of the air through the nostrils, the throat, and in the lungs. Be aware of the movement of your chest and abdomen as you breathe. Keep your undivided attention on your breath.

Do not attempt to change or control your breath in any way — simply observe it.

9. Sit. Relax. Imagine a circular pool of water in your mind. See it with your mind's eye. Imagine the pool being utterly still, without a ripple to disturb the surface. Hold your attention on keeping the surface still, imagining that any thoughts or distractions cause ripples or waves. When you find yourself thinking of anything else, smooth out the surface of the water again.

Keep the pool simple. Don't give it complicated edges or fish or water lilies, and let it reflect only a clear sky.

10. Sit. Relax. Visualise one of the quiet colours such as blue. Picture the blue shrinking down to a dot and then disappearing altogether, leaving your mind a blank. Stay completely blank. When you find yourself thinking of something, start again with the colour, and let it disappear into nothing.

This exercise is usually not recommended for beginners.

11. Sit. Relax. Count your breath: inhale (one), exhale (two), inhale (three), exhale (four), inhale (five), and so on as high as you can go in the predetermined practice time. Each time you lose count, simply start counting again.

Do not try to control your breath in any way.

12. Sit. Relax. Place a lighted candle in front of you. Observe the candle for one minute. Next, close your eyes and focus your attention on the movement of breath in your lower abdomen for one minute. Open your eyes and observe the candle again.

Keep alternating throughout the practice time, one minute for the candle, one minute for the breath.

Do not think profound thoughts about the meaning of the candle or anything else.

13. Sit. Relax. Place a lighted white candle in front of you. Gaze briefly at the candle and close your eyes. While your eyes are closed, visualise the candle. When you lose the inner image of the candle, look at it again, and then go back to the inner image. Don't strain your eyes.

Do not think about the symbolism of the candle. Keep your mind as blank as possible except for the image of the candle.

Practise spending increasing time with your eyes shut until you no longer need a physical candle. In this exercise, the candle is like waterwings for the beginning swimmer, and it should be dispensed with as soon as possible.

Alternative: Any other plain, uncomplicated object or any simple mandala (as described in Exercise 1) can also be used as a focus for concentration in the same manner as the candle.

14. Sit. Relax. Choose a small object, such as a marble or a plain ring — something which holds the eye and does not lead it away, yet is very simple. Place it just in front of you at about the level of your knees (on the floor if you are sitting on the floor). Keep your awareness on the object without thinking discursively about it.

After five minutes, move the object about 18 inches away from you. Observe. After another five minutes, move it another 18 inches away. Observe it for five minutes in that position.

In each position, only open your eyes enough to be able to see the object, so that you start with lowered eyelids, raising them and increasing your field of vision as you go, but retaining your focus on the object.

Throughout the meditation be aware of the movement of your breath in your lower abdomen.

15. Sit. Relax. Choose a subject for your receptive focus. Subjects such as compassion, faith, devotion, trust, integrity, honesty, love, and many others are suitable 'seeds' for the exercise. Do not think discursively about this subject. Just hold the concept in your mind and allow your thoughts to come and go. Because you are holding the subject in your

awareness, many of the thoughts which arise will be insights on that subject. Do not think about these insights, just be aware of them.

The same subject should be used for a number of sessions before going on another. It is also useful to return to a subject after a time and gain further insight. You may feel that you have all the insight possible in a short time, but this is more likely to be a manifestation of resistance rather than truth. The longer we hold a subject, the richer and deeper the insights tend to become — and often the longer it is between them.

16. Sit. Relax. Feel your pulse beat. Inhale to the count of six heartbeats, hold your breath for three beats, exhale during six beats, hold for another three. Repeat this cycle for the duration of your practice.

If you find difficulty in counting your heartbeats, just count as if you were counting seconds and ignore the heartbeat.

This exercise is advanced, and it should not be used unless other breath techniques have been practiced in the past.

17. Sit. Relax. Choose a word with positive and calming connotations, such as *peace, harmony, love, joy,* et cetera. Repeat this word over and over, either silently or aloud. If you do it aloud, let the sound rise up from your lower abdomen. Repeat your chosen word continuously during your practice period. Use the same word each time.

Do not analyse or think about or allow insights to arise about the meaning of the word.

This one is tricky — the choice of a suitable word can be difficult. Do not choose a word that presently is or is likely to be upsetting to you (e.g. if you feel very lonely or unloved, do not use love, *or if you feel very tense, do not use* relax). *To do so might only serve to call attention to the problem and set up unconscious resistance.*

18. Sit facing the wall. Relax. Look at the wall, observe it. Don't think about anything, just observe the wall. At the same time be aware of your breath.

Alternative: If you find it too difficult to think of nothing, you can count your breaths up to ten, then repeat.

Novices will find it easier to begin practising the exercise if they count the breaths.

19. Sit. Relax. Start saying AUM mentally. Make it one continuous sound and allow it to become fainter and fainter until it has faded entirely, leaving your mind a blank. Remain blank. When you become distracted, start again.

This exercise is usually not recommended for beginners.

20. Sit. Relax. Focus your awareness on a point of white light between your eyebrows. Keep your attention on that point of white light.

Alternative: Breathe into the point of white light between your eyebrows, until it fills and illumines the inside of your head. Gradually shift the focus of your awareness to the new centre of the white light in the centre of your head.

The alternative exercise is more suitable for an experienced meditator.

Appendix B

Reference Table

Exercise:	1	2	3	4	5	6	7	8	9	10	11	12	13	14	15	16	17	18	19	20
Inner	+	+	+	+	+	+	+	+	+	+	+	+	+	+	+	+	+	+	+	+
Outer		+										+	+	+			+			
Active	+	+	+		+	+	+	+	+	+	+	+	+	+	+	+	+	+	+	+
Passive				+										+						
Mental	+		+	+	+	*	+		+		+		+		+	+			+	+
Sensory		+	+			+	*	+			+	+				+		+		*
Visual	+			+					+	+			+							+
Non-Visual		+	+		+	+	+		*		+	+		+	+	+	+	+	+	
Will		+		+		*	+		+	+	+		+	+	+	+	*		+	+
Surrender		+	+	+		+		+			+	+			+	+				
Doing	+	+	+	+	+	+	+	+	+		+	+	+	+	+	+	+	+		+
Non-Doing										+									+	
Novice	+	+	+	+	+	*	+	+			+	+	+	+	+		+	*		*
Initiate	+	+	+	+	+	+	+	+	+	+	+	+	+	+	+	+	+	+	+	+

* Indicates that only one of the versions given fits this category.

Using This Table

You may have noticed above that some exercises contain elements of 'opposing' categories. In that case, we can expect it to have an integrating, balancing effect, and can use it to help balance ourselves.

Visual, in the table, means to visualise with the 'inner eye'. Some of the Non-Visual techniques may involve looking at something with the physical eyes.

Don't become too involved with this table. If it helps you, that's wonderful. If it confuses you, abandon it and simply use your intuition (another name for your inner teacher) to help you choose what is right for you. As mentioned earlier, none of these techniques will harm you — meditation has no undesirable side-effects as far as I know — and any of them are far, far better than not meditating.

Enjoy!

Notes

1 See 'The Physiology of Meditation" by R.K. Wallace & H. Benson in *Scientific American*, 1972, 226, No. 2, pp. 84-90.

2 See *Maximum Immunity* by Michael A. Weiner, PhD.. Gateway Books, 1986, p. 44.

3 Quoted from O. Sogen and T. Katsujo in *Zen and the Art of Calligraphy*. Translated by John Stevens. Routledge & Kegan Paul, 1983, p. 54.

4 For a comprehensive discussion of hypnosis written for the layman, see *Self-Hypnotism* by Leslie LeCron.

5 Quoted from the Bible, I Corinthians, 13: 4-7. Revised Standard Version. William Collins.

6 See 'Intangibles in Medicine" by Norman Cousins, M.D. in the *Journal of the American Medical Association*. 16 September, 1988; *260, No. 11;* pp 1610-1612. Also see *Maximum Immunity* by Michael A. Weiner, PhD., and *Loving Medicine* by Rosy Thomson, M.B., including Chapter 9 by Michael Wetzler, M.D., on 'The Mind and Cancer: Causation and Therapy". Gateway Books, 1989.

7 See 'Micromotion of the Body as a Factor in the Development of the Nervous System" by I. Bentov, in *Kundalini: Evolution & Enlightenment*. Edited by John White. Pp. 316-339.

8 For a more extensive discussion of Zen, Zazen, and *shikan-taza*, see the *The Three Pillars of Zen* by Roshi P. Kapleau. Rider, 1985.

References

Anonymous. *The Cloud of Unknowing and Other Works*. Translated into modern English by Clifton Wolters. Penguin, 1987.

Cade, C.M., & Coxhead, N. *The Awakened Mind*. Element Books, 1987.

Cousins, N. "Intangibles in Medicine" in the *Journal of the American Medical Association*. 16 September, 1988; 260, No. 11; pp 1610-1612.

Happold, F.C., Editor. Mysticism: *A Study and an Anthology*. Penguin, 1963.

Holmes, Stewart W., & Horioka, Chimyo. *Zen Art for Meditation*. Charles E. Tuttle Company, 1988.

Houston, Jean. *The Possible Human*. J.P. Tarcher, Inc., 1982.

Johnston, William. *Silent Music: The Science of Meditation*. William Collins (Fount Paperbacks), 1985.

Kapleau, P. *The Three Pillars of Zen*. Rider, 1985.

Khosla, K. *The Sufism of Rumi*. Element Books, 1987.

Naranjo, C., & Ornstein, R.E. *On the Psychology of Meditation*. Viking Press, 1971.

Sekida, Katsuki. *Zen Training: Methods and Philosophy*. Weatherhill, Inc., 1985.

Shah, I. *The Way of the Sufi*. Penguin, 1986.

Sogen, O., & Katsujo, T. *Zen and the Art of Calligraphy*. Translated by John Stevens. London: Routledge & Kegan Paul, 1983.

Tart, Charles T. *States of Consciousness*. New York: E.P. Dutton, 1975.
  — Editor. Altered States of Consciousness. New York: John Wiley, 1969.

Thomas á Kempis. *The Imitation of Christ*. Hodder & Stoughton, 1977.

Thomson, R. *Loving Medicine*. Gateway Books, 1989

Weiner, Michael A. *Maximum Immunity*. Gateway Books, 1986.

Welch, John. *Spiritual Pilgrims: Carl Jung and Teresa of Avila*. Paulist Press, 1982.

White, J., Editor. *Kundalini, Evolution and Enlightenment*. Anchor Books/ Doubleday, 1979.

Companion Tapes to *Moon Over Water*

Letting Go: *Breathing into Deep Space*
Two imagery exercises to guide you to deep relaxation for the restoration of mind, body and spirit. *(45 mins. each side: £8.95 incl. UK post)*

Centering: *Finding the place of Inner Power*
These earthing and centering exercises are suitable for anyone finding themselves scattered or drained by others' energies. *(30 mins. each side: £7.95 incl. UK post)*

Embracing Healing: *Deep Self-Healing*
These exercises focus on healing of mind and body through the conscious use of natural healing energy and affirmations. *(30 mins. each side: £7.95 incl. UK post)*

Do you know about Jessica's other book **Sun Over Mountain?** It is the companion to **Moon Over Water,** and it teaches us to use imagery to heal ourselves, change old ways and transform our lives. Muz Murray says: "It is the most fulfilling book of creative visualisation I have encountered. It is inspiring to read and even more to practise. You will journey with a very sympathetic guide who well knows the way."

288 pages £8.95 (£1 UK post)

Companion Tapes to *Sun Over Mountain*

Taking Care: *The Healing of Body, Mind and Spirit*
These imagery journeys help us to improve our capacity for healing and enhancing the natural body/mind healing process. *(30 mins. each side: £7.95 incl. post)*

Focusing In: *Enhancing Self-transformation*
These imagery journeys take us deep into ourselves, helping us to create change at deep levels. *(45 mins. each side: £8.95 incl. post)*

Expanding Out: *The Flowering of Consciousness*
These are journeys to enhance the expansion of consciousness in which we experience new ways of being and facilitate self-transformation. *(45 mins. each side: £8.95 incl. post)*

Would you like to know about other self-transforming books published by Gateway? Write for our catalogue today, to:
Gateway Books, The Hollies, Wellow, Bath BA2 8QJ.
In the USA: Gateway Books, 17470 Sonoma Highway, Sonoma, CA 95476